AF510042

THE GLOBAL PHARMACY RETAIL LANDSCAPE: INSIGHTS FROM 79 NATIONS

Sujit Paul

notionpress.com
INDIA • SINGAPORE • MALAYSIA

ISBN

Paperback 979-8-90296-446-9
Hardcase 979-8-90342-669-0

Global Retail Pharmacy Market Preface

A Personal Note from the Group CEO

Over the years, I have read and initiated many global pharmaceutical overviews. Most of them were thorough. Many were carefully researched, supported by data, charts, and regulatory summaries. And yet, when it came time to make real decisions, where to invest, where to pull back, where to take risks, very few of those documents truly helped.

The reason is straightforward. Most global overviews organise the world by maps. They describe continents, regions, and countries as if geography itself explains behaviour. In practice, it rarely does.

Pharmaceutical markets do not operate neatly by continent. They operate according to how rules are enforced, how medicines are paid for, how quickly patients can actually be reached, and how costly mistakes turn out to be.

Markets separated by thousands of kilometres can feel remarkably similar once you are operating on the ground. At the same time, neighbouring countries, often grouped in strategy decks, can require completely different approaches.

This overview is written to reflect that lived reality. It is not meant to be encyclopedic. It is intended to be useful.

Global Retail Pharmacy Market Overview

The global retail pharmacy market plays a central role in the distribution of medicinal products and health-related goods, serving as the primary point of contact between patients and pharmacotherapy.

This presents a comprehensive overview of the structure, scale, and evolving dynamics of retail pharmacy markets worldwide, drawing on recent industry data, macro-economic health spending patterns, and workforce insights.

Retail pharmacy encompasses brick-and-mortar stores, chain and independent outlets, and increasingly, digital and ePharmacy platforms.

While the core activity remains the dispensing of prescription and over-the-counter (OTC) medicines, many pharmacies now deliver broader services including education, vaccination, chronic disease support, and wellness products.

Country-Wise Retail Pharma Market Summaries

Portugal – Pharmaceutical Retail Market Summary (2025)

Market Size & Growth

- Portugal's pharmaceutical market is projected to reach between USD 2.1 and USD 2.5 billion by end of 2025; the total pharma and OTC market stands at approximately USD 4.9 billion.
- Generics currently make up over 40% of prescriptions and are growing due to legislative price controls requiring generics to be at least 50% lower than bran ded originals.
- Recent public investments have focused on digital health, e-prescription adoption, and infrastructure, yet the SNS faces financial deficits, sustaining cost pressures and slowly increasing private health insurance uptake.

Market Structure

- The retail network includes over 2,800 community pharmacies, with pharmacies remaining the primary channel for consumer healthcare and generics.
- The market features a mix of multinationals (such as Pfizer, Merck, and Johnson & Johnson), local manufacturers (Bial, Bluepharma, Hovione), wholesalers, and a strong hospital sector.
- INFARMED (National Medicines Authority) oversees all approvals, reimbursement, and regulatory standards, aligned with the EU framework.

ePrescription and Digital Health

- Portugal launched ePrescription in 2015, and today 97%+ of all prescriptions are digital, available via app, SMS, or email, with cross-border interoperability enabling EU citizens to use e-prescriptions in Portugal.
- Digital health expansion includes electronic health records and telemedicine, further modernizing access and patient experience.

Market Dynamics

- An aging population, rising chronic disease, and strong universal healthcare system drive prescription drug demand.
- Cost-containment policies, reference pricing, and copay systems support high generic drug use but create reimbursement delays and regulatory complexity.

Consumer Behaviour

- Portuguese consumers prefer pharmacies for generics and personal health care; trust in pharmacists is high.
- Online pharmacy and personalized medicine are rising trends, accentuated by pandemic-related shifts to e-commerce.

Key Drivers

- Demand for generics, health awareness, digital health, and government investment in patient care innovation and technology.

Key Challenges

- Slow reimbursement timetables, workforce shortages, intellectual property complexity, and market lag compared to EU peers.

Opportunities

- Biotech innovation, advanced drug delivery platforms, clinical trial ecosystem growth, public-private partnerships, and further generic uptake in hospital and outpatient care.

Regulatory Environment

- INFARMED controls pricing, reimbursement, approvals, and pharmacovigilance, with most applications for generics streamlining via abbreviated procedures for EU-aligned products.
- Reference pricing and demand-side incentives for physicians and pharmacists drive generic use, with supply-side regulatory focus on minimum price gaps.

Strategic Considerations

- Cultivate partnerships in biotech, clinical trials, and eHealth.

Gabon – Pharmaceutical Retail Market Summary (2025)

Market Size & Growth

- Gabon's pharmaceutical market is projected to reach USD 45.19 million in 2025 with annual growth rates averaging between 4% and 6%.
- Prescription drugs, particularly for oncology and chronic diseases, form the largest segment; additional pharmaceutical revenue (other categories) is forecasted at USD 18.38 million.
- Gabon's pharmaceutical imports reached USD 110–119 million in 2023, indicating continued reliance on foreign medicines and moderate market expansion.

Market Structure

- The country's pharmacy network includes both independent and small chain pharmacies; large chains have increased recent expansion to meet rising demand.
- Distribution is regulated by the Directorate of Medicine and Pharmacy under the Ministry of Health, with both public and private wholesalers and pharmacies subject to annual inspections.

ePrescription and Digital Health

- A national electronic health information system (HIS) is being deployed to connect health institutions and providers, aiming to improve medicine management and pave the way for ePrescription adoption.

Market Dynamics

- Growth is driven by increasing healthcare awareness, chronic disease, and aging population.
- Challenges include infrastructural limitations, regulatory delays, budget constraints, and persistent risk of counterfeit medicines.

Consumer Behaviour

- Patients increasingly rely on pharmacies for prescription medicines, with convenience and variety contributing to market growth.
- Urbanization and health education efforts are influencing consumer preferences toward formally regulated pharmacy channels.

Key Drivers

- Population growth, gradual expansion of health insurance coverage, ongoing digital health initiatives, and evolving regulatory compliance.

Key Challenges

- Import dependency, regulatory enforcement gaps, limited local manufacturing, and supply chain inefficiencies.

Opportunities

- Infrastructure improvements, pharmacy chain expansion, digitalization, public-private partnerships, and regulatory harmonization with WHO and African Medicines Agency standards.

Regulatory Environment

- Directorate of Medicine and Pharmacy (Ministry of Health) manages registration, inspection, licensing, import control, and annual inspections.
- Gabon collaborates with WHO and regional bodies to strengthen GMP, pharmacovigilance, and safety oversight.

Strategic Considerations

- Invest in healthcare infrastructure, digital health integration, quality assurance, and compliance.
- Develop distribution and supply chain partnerships to improve medicine access and combat counterfeiting.

South Korea – Pharmaceutical Retail Market Summary (2025)

Market Size & Growth

- South Korea's total pharmaceutical market reached approximately USD 22.3 billion in 2023, with generics accounting for ~55% of prescriptions and 35–40% of market value.
- The retail generics segment for 2025 is estimated at USD 6.5–7.2 billion, growing at a CAGR of 4.8% through 2029; rising to about USD 10.2 billion by 2033.
- Key growth drivers include an aging population, widespread National Health Insurance (NHI), and continuous cost control policies.

Market Structure

- Dominated by urban retail pharmacy chains (e.g., Onnuri, Pharmstrong), hospital-linked dispensaries, and strong local manufacturers such as Hanmi, Daewoong, Chong Kun Dang, and Yuhan.
- Most generics are produced domestically; OTC retail is led by platforms like Coupang Health and Olive Young.
- Hospital vs. retail pharmacy fragmentation persists; pharmacies face reimbursement margin pressures.

ePrescription and Digital Health

- ePharmacy for prescription drugs is limited with select OTC and quasi-drugs allowed; e-prescribing and telepharmacy pilots are present but tightly regulated.
- Electronic Health Record (EHR) adoption is increasing but trails major international benchmarks due to limited interoperability and cost barriers.

Consumer Behaviour

- Korean consumers demonstrate high trust in domestically-made generics, strong urban eCommerce use for OTC/supplements, and loyalty to community and hospital pharmacies..

Key Drivers

- Aging population (25% aged 65+ by 2025), chronic disease rates, robust domestic manufacturing capacity, NHI generic substitution policies, high digital adoption for health/eCommerce.

Key Challenges

- Prescription eCommerce restrictions, system fragmentation between hospital and retail pharmacies, regulatory complexity (patent linkage, price reform, manufacturing standards), margin pressure, and occasional delays in reimbursement.

Opportunities

- Mobile OTC/wellness retail, branded generics, chronic disease management, private-label products via major pharmacy chains, and increased use of digital tools for consumer engagement.

Regulatory Environment

- Regulated by the Ministry of Health and Welfare (MOHW) and Ministry of Food and Drug Safety (MFDS); generics require bioequivalence not full clinical trials.
- Rx ePharmacy faces tight restrictions, while OTC online sales permitted; patent linkage affects generic market entry timing.

Strategic Considerations

- Focus on NHI formulary-aligned generics, strategic partnerships with leading retail chains, digital subscription/diagnostics bundles for chronic therapeutic areas, and regulatory compliance for bioequivalence and safety.

Turkmenistan – Pharmaceutical Retail Market Summary (2025)

Market Size & Growth

- Turkmenistan's pharmaceutical market value stands at approximately USD 379 million in 2025, with an annual growth rate around 6%.
- Imports account for over 90% of medicines, supplied mainly by India, Russia, and Iran.
- Local manufacturing is expanding gradually-major initiatives include Saglyk and Turkmendermansenagat, but import reliance is still dominant.

Market Structure

- The retail landscape is dominated by state-owned pharmacies managed by the Ministry of Health; private pharmacies exist but are concentrated in major cities like Ashgabat.
- Centralized distribution is managed by Turkmendermansenagat, covering procurement, warehousing, and logistics.
- OTC drug sales are increasing rapidly, with the segment projected to reach USD 410 million by 2025.

ePrescription and Digital Health

- E-prescription adoption is very low, and digital health infrastructure is still at an early phase, focused primarily on centralized health information systems.
- Government priorities include tracking systems for medicine traceability and efforts to reduce counterfeit risks as digitalization evolves.

Market Dynamics

- Prescription drugs for chronic and specialty diseases (e.g., oncology, diabetes) are a key segment; oncology drug sales are projected at USD 70 million for 2025.
- Price controls, advertising bans, and currency volatility affect supply chain stability and cause periodic shortages.

Consumer Behaviour

- Urban residents have greater pharmacy access; rural areas depend heavily on state channels.
- Herbal and traditional medicines see increasing popularity alongside generics.

Key Drivers

- Government investment in health, growth in chronic illness, prevention efforts, and widespread health education initiatives.

Key Challenges

- Persistent import reliance, supply chain disruptions, regulatory complexity, limited private sector development, and skills gaps in pharmaceutical operations.

Opportunities

- Local manufacturing partnerships, digital health expansion, supply chain modernization, and broader product mix in both generics and traditional medicines.

Regulatory Environment

- Ministry of Health and Medical Industry oversees regulation, drug registration, and quality control, with support from the State Sanitary and Epidemiological Surveillance Service.
- International collaboration and training are improving regulatory standards, with alignment to WHO and EMA practices underway.

Strategic Considerations

- Leverage local partnerships and government relationships for market entry.
- Emphasize compliance, cost competitiveness, and portfolio diversity.
- Invest in supply chain resilience and digital upgrades for traceability and efficiency.

TAIWAN – PHARMACEUTICAL RETAIL MARKET SUMMARY (2025)

Market Size & Growth

- Taiwan's pharmacy retail market is projected to reach USD 4.6 billion by 2025, with revenue growth expected to continue at a CAGR of 8.3% through 2031.
- Generics and patented drugs both have significant shares, but generics are gaining in market importance due to cost controls and insurance reimbursement systems.
- Growth is driven by universal insurance coverage, rising chronic disease rates, consumer demand for convenience, and expansion of organized pharmacy chains.

Market Structure

- Around 8,100 pharmacy outlets operate nationwide, mostly independent but with a growing presence of organized chains such as MedFirst, Great Tree Pharmacy, TinTin Drugstores, and YourChance Pharmacy.
- Chains are expanding via new stores and M&A; customers favor independent stores for NHI-accredited prescriptions, while chains focus on non-pharma products for revenue.
- The organized sector is increasing market share via technology integration, membership schemes, and service expansion.

ePrescription and Digital Health

- Taiwan has advanced e-prescription and EHR digitalization; >90% of medical records are digitalized in large hospitals.
- Online pharmacies are rapidly expanding, now valued at USD 65 billion in 2025 with a projected CAGR of 18.6% to 2031; trends include AI-driven prescription management and strong telemedicine integration.
- Regulatory frameworks are evolving to improve digital safety, prescription validation, and patient privacy.

Market Dynamics

- Prescribed medicines (especially for chronic disease) remain the largest product segment, but demand for OTC and wellness products is rising.
- Market growth is supported by preventative health trends, aging population, government reforms, and digital transformation.

Consumer Behaviour

- Consumers show strong trust in pharmacists and prefer affordable generics for maintenance and chronic therapies.
- Digital adoption for online ordering and home delivery is rising, especially in urban regions.

Key Drivers

- Universal insurance coverage, chronic disease rise, e-health platforms, chain pharmacy expansion, and increasing healthcare expenditures.

Key Challenges

- Price competition, fragmented regulation, counterfeiting risks with online sales, slow new drug launch timelines due to complex approvals, persistent dominance of unorganized sector in store numbers.

Opportunities

- Digital health and e-pharmacy growth, partnerships in chronic disease management, expansion of preventive health and wellness services, integration with telemedicine platforms.

Regulatory Environment

- Taiwan Food and Drug Administration (TFDA) oversees approvals, post-market surveillance, clinical trials, and GMP compliance.

Strategic Considerations

- Invest in digital integration, patient engagement, and product portfolio expansion.
- Align business models with NHI reimbursement structure and regulatory best practices.

Denmark – Pharmaceutical Retail Market Summary (2025)

Market Size & Growth

- The Denmark pharmaceutical market is projected at USD 4.05 billion in 2025, growing at a CAGR of 3.28% and expected to reach USD 4.76 billion by 2030; some estimates range up to USD 5.2 billion by 2033.
- Generics comprise 46% of prescriptions by volume and 18% by value in ambulatory care, reflecting strong uptake.
- Growth is supported by healthcare digitization, aging population, chronic disease prevalence, and heavy R&D investment from leading companies like Novo Nordisk and Lundbeck.

Market Structure

- 514 licensed community pharmacies operate under strict ownership laws; generics are dispensed via national substitution lists managed by the Danish Medicines Agency (DKMA).
- Online pharmacies are licensed, OTC is sold in compliant non-pharmacy venues, and the system is built on national e-prescription infrastructure (>95% coverage).

ePrescription and Digital Health

- Denmark is a global leader in e-prescribing; nearly 100% primary care prescriptions are issued and processed electronically, fully integrated for repeat orders, home delivery, and pharmacist counseling.
- Community pharmacies provide digital ordering and delivery services for both Rx and OTC.

Market Dynamics

- Reference pricing policies and reimbursement clusters guide dispensing toward lowest-cost generics; margin pressures and supply constraints occasionally affect availability.
- High digital adoption, strong preventive health orientation, and consistent self-care and OTC sales contribute to sector resilience.

Consumer Behaviour

- Strong bioequivalence standards, widespread pharmacist counseling, and high digital literacy drive acceptance of generics and e-health services.
- Customers regularly use digital resources for prescription management.

Key Drivers

- Aging population, rising chronic illnesses, mature digital prescription network, R&D innovation, and robust government support underpin sustained market expansion.

Key Challenges

- Price regulation, occasional supply constraints, compensation system limiting revenue growth, workforce and operating cost pressures.

Opportunities for New Entrants

- Chronic therapy generics aligned with substitution lists, private-label OTC, advanced digital fulfillment, and clinical wellness diversification.

Regulatory Environment

- Danish Medicines Agency (DKMA) regulates authorization, reimbursement, substitution lists, and pharmacovigilance under the Danish Medicines Act.
- Licensed e-pharmacies are subject to strict online sale verification and regulatory requirements.

Strategic Considerations

- Align product portfolio to substitution clusters and reference pricing systems.
- Invest in automation, clinical services, and digital solutions to enhance margin and fulfillment.
- Diversify into OTC wellness and clinical adjacencies for growth beyond reimbursed prescriptions.

Tunisia – Pharmaceutical Retail Market Summary (2025)

Market Size & Growth

- Tunisia's pharmaceutical market was valued at approximately USD 2.15 billion in 2023 and is projected to grow at a CAGR of 12.9% from 2024 to 2030, reaching nearly USD 5.03 billion.
- Local generic drug production accounts for about 49%, with imports comprising the remaining 51%.
- Growth is driven by developed pharmaceutical infrastructure, skilled workforce, rising healthcare demand, and government promotion of local manufacturing.

Market Structure

- Tunisia has around 39 pharmaceutical companies mainly clustered in regions including Tunis, Sfax, and Sousse.
- The sector features a mix of local producers, joint ventures with multinationals, and significant imports from neighboring countries.
- The pharmaceutical distribution is state-controlled through the Central Pharmacy of Tunisia, ensuring secure and monitored supply chains.

ePrescription and Digital Health

- The country is advancing digital health with telemedicine regulations established in 2022, enhancing remote consultations especially in underserved regions.
- Electronic Common Technical Document (eCTD) format for pharmaceutical submissions is being fully implemented by 2026 to streamline regulatory processes.
- National telemedicine adoption faces legal and infrastructure challenges but holds significant growth potential.

Market Dynamics

- The market is propelled by government investment, expanding middle class, and increasing prevalence of chronic diseases.
- Pricing reforms and reimbursement policies aim to contain healthcare expenditures, with the government subsidizing high-cost innovative drugs.
- Digitalization trends are driving new business models, including e-pharmacies and enhanced supply chain management.

Consumer Behaviour

- Patients show growing preference for generics and OTC products; access disparities between urban and rural areas persist.
- Digital engagement is emerging but constrained by uneven access to technology.

Key Drivers

- Strong R&D, government incentives for generics and biosimilars, export initiatives, and regional integration boost market growth.

Key Challenges

- Price pressures on low-cost drugs, intermittent medicine shortages, and regulatory reform delays impact sector stability.
- Need for legislative action to regulate non-drug health products and enhance quality control.

Opportunities for New Entrants

- Expansion of generic medicine manufacturing and export.
- Digital health services, telepharmacy, and innovative therapies.
- Strategic partnerships with local firms and public health programs.

Regulatory Environment

- The Directorate of Pharmacy and Medicine (DPM) governs pharmaceuticals registration, quality assurance, and supervision.

Strategic Considerations

- Emphasize regulatory compliance and quality assurance to strengthen market position.
- Invest in digital transformation for pharmacy services and patient outreach.

Senegal – Pharmaceutical Retail Market Summary (2025)

Market Size & Growth

- Senegal's pharmaceutical market is growing steadily, valued near USD 600 million in 2024 and projected to expand at a CAGR of approximately 7.5% through 2030.
- Increasing healthcare expenditure, population growth, and rising demand for both generics and innovative medicines support market expansion.
- Local government initiatives focus on improving medicine accessibility and promoting local pharmaceutical manufacturing.

Market Structure

- The market consists mainly of standalone pharmacies in urban and peri-urban areas; chain pharmacies are emerging but not yet dominant.
- Private wholesalers supply most of the market; roughly 85-90% of medicines are imported, with limited domestic manufacturing.
- The state controls parts of the distribution chain through the National Drug Supply Agency (ANSD), facilitating essential medicine availability.

ePrescription and Digital Health

- Digital health infrastructure is nascent but developing, with increasing adoption of e-prescription systems and telemedicine services, especially post-pandemic.
- Regulatory frameworks support digital transformation, though rural regions face infrastructural challenges.

Market Dynamics

- Drivers include a growing middle class, urbanization, increased prevalence of non-communicable diseases, and government healthcare reforms.
- Challenges include counterfeit medicines, regulatory enforcement gaps, limited healthcare access in rural areas, and economic constraints.

Consumer Behaviour

- Consumers show increasing preference for affordable generic medicines; pharmacies commonly serve as first-access healthcare providers.
- Traditional medicine use remains culturally significant alongside formal pharmaceuticals.

Key Drivers

- Population growth, expanding health insurance coverage, public-private partnerships, and donor-funded health programs stimulate pharmaceutical demand.

Key Challenges

- Regulatory inconsistencies, counterfeit drug circulation, infrastructure limitations, and dependency on imports create obstacles.

Opportunities

- Expansion of local manufacturing capabilities, investment in supply chain modernization, uptake of digital health innovations, and public-private collaborations.

Regulatory Environment

- Senegal's medicines regulation is overseen by the Department of Pharmacy and Laboratories (DPL) with international alignment via WHO and AMRH initiatives.
- Senegal became the first Francophone African country to reach WHO Maturity Level 3 (ML3) for medicines regulation, indicating a stable and effective regulatory system.

Strategic Considerations

- Strengthen regulatory enforcement and quality assurance to combat counterfeit medicines.
- Invest in digital infrastructure to enhance pharmacy services and patient access.
- Leverage Senegal's emerging role as a regional pharmaceutical and vaccine production hub for growth and innovation.

Ethiopia – Pharmaceutical Retail Market Summary (2025)

Market Size & Growth

- Ethiopia's pharmaceutical market has experienced rapid growth over the past decade, valued at around USD 800–900 million recently, with a projected reach of USD 1.8 billion by 2025 and USD 3.6 billion by 2030.
- The market is growing at an estimated CAGR of around 11.3% to 17.5% (2025–2029) with oral solid dosage forms (tablets, capsules) comprising over 75% of the market by volume.
- Imports constitute approximately 80–85% of pharmaceuticals, primarily sourced from India, Netherlands, and Belgium. Local production capacity remains limited but is expanding through government-supported industrial parks.

Market Structure

- Ethiopia's pharmaceutical sector includes public and private players: Ethiopian Pharmaceutical Supply Agency (EPSA) dominates public sector procurement and distribution, while private sector covers 44% of the market.
- Retail pharmacies, hospital pharmacies, and informal drug vendors serve urban and rural populations, with regulatory systems evolving to formalize and improve quality standards.

ePrescription and Digital Health

- E-prescription and electronic health records are in nascent stages; factors influencing adoption include perceived ease of use, trust, and technology self-efficacy among healthcare providers.
- Digital adoption is uneven, and paper-based prescriptions remain common.
- Pilot programs and technology acceptance studies indicate increasing willingness to shift to electronic systems over time.

Market Dynamics

- Major drug categories include anti-infectives, gastrointestinal, cardiovascular, and CNS drugs, driving governmental and private demand.
- Government incentives focus on import tariff protection, procurement reforms, and industrial park investments for pharmaceutical manufacturing.

Consumer Behaviour

- Affordability and accessibility influence consumer preferences; local manufacturers are trusted when quality is assured.

Key Drivers

- Rising population, urbanization, government health programs, and growing chronic disease burden fuel demand.

Key Challenges

- Regulatory enforcement gaps, limited inter-agency cooperation, foreign currency shortages impacting imports, and counterfeit drug circulation remain major challenges.
- Quality control and formalization of drug retail are ongoing priorities.

Opportunities

- Scaling local manufacturing capacity, strengthening supply chain transparency, expanding digital health infrastructure, and improving regulatory harmonization.

Regulatory Environment

- Ethiopian Food and Drug Authority (EFDA) leads medicine registration and regulation; part of regional harmonization initiatives (EAC, IGAD).

Strategic Considerations

- Invest in technology acceptance and training for e-prescribing systems.
- Develop quality assurance and counterfeit mitigation strategies.
- Support public-private partnerships to improve manufacturing and distribution.

Albania – Pharmaceutical Retail Market Summary (2025)

Market Size & Growth

- Albania's pharmaceutical market is projected at approximately USD 88.64 million in 2025, growing at a CAGR of 4.99% to reach about USD 113 million by 2030.
- Generics make up around 76% of consumption, with innovative therapies accounting for 24%. Growth is driven by rising health awareness, economic growth, and healthcare reforms.

Market Structure

- Over 1,000 pharmacies and 200 pharmaceutical warehouses operate, mainly standalone with increasing chain consolidation.
- Imports dominate from Turkey, Germany, Italy, Switzerland, Hungary; local manufacturers like Rejsi Farma, Galaxy Pharma growing modestly.

ePrescription and Digital Health

- Partial e-prescription adoption since 2017 through the e-Albania portal, currently covering 9 of 12 regions; challenges include infrastructure and training gaps.
- The system reduces prescription errors and administrative burdens with ongoing national rollout plans.

Market Dynamics

- Driven by aging population, chronic disease prevalence, healthcare spending increases.
- Pricing and reimbursement policies control access; out-of-pocket costs remain significant (~€160 million in 2024).
- Trends in digitalization and consolidation affect pharmacy services and customer experiences.

Consumer Behaviour

- Growing preference for affordable generics and self-care OTC products.
- Emerging but limited online pharmacy and digital health engagement.

Key Drivers

- Economic growth, government reforms aligned with EU, and expanding middle class boost demand.
- Healthcare infrastructure and regulatory advancements strengthen market.

Key Challenges

- Regulatory capacity constraints, fragmented market, financial access barriers, and limited import quality checks.

Opportunities

- Expansion in generic manufacturing, digital pharmacy innovation, specialty therapies.
- Collaborations with healthcare institutions enhance service innovation.

Regulatory Environment

- National Agency of Pharmaceuticals and Medical Devices (AKMS) oversees approval, quality control, and compliance with increasing alignment to EU GMP/GDP.
- Reforms improve clinical trial evaluation and pharmacovigilance standards.

Strategic Considerations

- Prioritize compliance and quality to build trust.
- Invest in digitalization and patient engagement.
- Leverage incentives for local production and market growth.

Mali – Pharmaceutical Retail Market Summary (2025)

Market Size & Growth

- Import-dependent, with medicinal and pharmaceutical product imports valued at approximately USD 43.3 million in 2023, showing steady growth.
- Retail and generic pharmaceutical segments are projected to grow moderately through 2025-2031.
- The broader Middle East and Africa generic drug market is forecasted to grow at a CAGR of 6.6% from 2025 to 2033, influencing Mali's market prospects.

Market Structure

- Market comprises mainly standalone pharmacies in urban areas; local manufacturing is limited, and imports dominate supply chains.
- Distribution is fragmented; ongoing public-private partnerships seek to strengthen supply chain and medicine accessibility.
- Informal sector and counterfeit medicines remain significant challenges.

ePrescription and Digital Health

- Electronic prescription adoption is minimal, constrained by infrastructure and regulatory development.
- Pilot programs exist for digital health record and e-prescribing system implementation, indicating future growth potential.

Market Dynamics

- Challenges include low healthcare expenditure, infrastructure gaps, and economic constraints.
- Disease burden from infectious and non-communicable diseases drives demand for affordable generics.
- Regional integration (AMRH) and international support boost regulatory improvements and supply chain strengthening.

Consumer Behaviour

- High price sensitivity; generics favored due to affordability.
- Medication safety awareness growing, limited in rural populations by education and access issues.

Key Drivers

- Growing chronic disease prevalence, governmental health priorities, and international partnerships.
- India's pharmaceutical exports to Mali valued at nearly USD 30 million in 2023 provide critical supply support.

Key Challenges

- Weak local production capabilities, counterfeit medicine prevalence (55-60%), and regulatory complexities.
- Administrative and infrastructural barriers limit efficient market expansion.

Opportunities for New Entrants

- Expanding import and distribution of generics; scaling local pharmaceutical manufacturing.
- Digital health infrastructure investments and pharmacist training programs offer growth areas.

Regulatory Environment

- Directorate of Pharmacy and Medicine oversees registration and market authorization; quality control by National Health Laboratory.
- Mali aligns with WHO, ECOWAS, and UEMOA regulatory frameworks; working on tightening counterfeit controls and pharmacy regulation formalization.

Strategic Considerations

- Forge partnerships with local distributors and pharmacies for regulatory navigation.
- Enhance supply chain transparency to combat counterfeit drugs.
- Leverage regional harmonization efforts to improve market access and compliance.

CHAD – PHARMACEUTICAL RETAIL MARKET SUMMARY (2025)

Market Size & Growth

- Chad's pharmaceutical market is projected to reach approximately US$64.67 million in 2025, with an expected steady growth driven by rising demand for affordable medications.
- Oncology drugs represent a significant segment with a forecasted revenue of US$7.05 million in 2025.
- The pharmaceuticals market has a modest CAGR of 1.3% projected through 2028 amid low healthcare infrastructure and economic challenges.

Market Structure

- The pharmacy sector is primarily composed of small, standalone pharmacies concentrated in urban centers, with very limited chain presence.
- Approximately 90% of pharmaceutical products are imported, highlighting a major dependency on foreign suppliers including India and

European countries.

- Public sector medicines are distributed through the Pharmaceutical Purchasing Centre (CPA), aiming to coordinate essential drug supply.
- Local manufacturing is negligible; efforts are ongoing to explore establishing drug manufacturing capabilities.

ePrescription and Digital Health

- ePrescription adoption is minimal due to infrastructural and regulatory constraints; handwritten prescriptions remain standard.
- Healthcare ICT development is under early stages, with pilot programs initiated for digital health record implementation.
- Digital prescribing has significant potential but requires government commitment and infrastructure scaling.

Market Dynamics

- Economic constraints, unstable political environment, and limited healthcare facilities affect consistent pharmaceutical supply.
- Retail pharmacies serve as the primary medicine access points for urban and peri-urban populations.

Consumer Behaviour

- Consumers strongly prefer affordable generic medicines due to low-income levels; traditional medicine remains widely used in rural areas.

Key Drivers

- Demand growth is spurred by rising prevalence of infectious and non-communicable diseases (e.g., malaria, diabetes), and government health initiatives.

Key Challenges

- Severe shortages of qualified pharmacists (approx. 1 per 300,000 inhabitants) and inadequate healthcare infrastructure.
- Lack of local pharmaceutical production raises dependency on imports and exposure to supply disruptions.

Opportunities for New Entrants

- Expansion of generic drug importation and distribution networks.
- Investment in local manufacturing facilities for essential medicines, addressing supply gaps.

Regulatory Environment

- Ministry of Public Health regulates pharmaceutical imports, pricing, and quality control.
- Chad ratified the African Medicines Agency (AMA) treaty in 2021, signaling moves toward regional regulatory harmonization and capacity building.

Strategic Considerations

- Prioritize establishing supply chain resilience through public-private partnerships.
- Develop affordable generics and strengthen regulatory compliance capabilities.

Georgia – Pharmaceutical Retail Market Summary (2025)

Market Size & Growth

- Pharmaceutical market revenue is projected to reach US$135 million in 2025, with generics playing a key role in meeting public health and cost containment needs.
- The sector is expanding on rising healthcare expenditures, an aging population, and a high prevalence of chronic diseases.
- Steady growth is forecast due to investments in healthcare infrastructure, policy reforms, and a shift toward personalized medicine and biotechnology.

Market Structure

- Georgia's retail pharmacy landscape features a mix of multinational chains and domestic companies, large retail banners, and independent pharmacies.
- Chain pharmacies are expanding, but local businesses remain significant, especially outside the main cities.
- Both prescription and OTC drugs show strong demand due to chronic disease and increased wellness awareness.

eCommerce and Digital Health

- E-prescribing systems are available for controlled substances, minimizing wait times and improving dispensing speed and safety.
- Georgia participated in the first EU4Digital cross-border ePrescription test in 2024, enabling international Rx data exchange and improving access for EU travelers.
- Growth of telemedicine, e-pharmacies, and digital distribution accelerates as the healthcare environment modernizes.

Market Dynamics

- Market is competitive, facing strong price pressure, challenges in rural access, and persistent issues of counterfeit drugs.
- Government initiatives support generic prescribing, price control, and improved medication access.

Consumer Behaviour

- Increasing consumer awareness in health and wellness; high demand for insurance reimbursement and affordable medication access, especially for branded generics.
- Patient demand is shifting to specialty medicines, biotech, and personalized therapies as new products become available.

Key Drivers

- Government policies, investments in infrastructure, and rising incidence of chronic and rare diseases fuel market expansion and generic adoption.
- Initiatives like the national health insurance program and pricing controls make generics more accessible.

Key Challenges

- Regulatory compliance, rural access, and competition, plus concerns about counterfeit drugs and intellectual property.

Opportunities for New Entrants

- Investment in digital health, e-pharmacies, chronic care management, and specialty generics.
- Strong demand for affordable generics and modern retail formats across both urban and rural communities.

Regulatory and Strategic Considerations

- State Regulatory Agency oversees drug approvals, pricing, and compliance.
- Government aims to improve access via reimbursement and insurance programs, prioritizing safety and affordability.
- Strategic partnerships and digital channel development are key to expanding market presence.

United Arab Emirates – Pharmaceutical Retail Market Summary (2025)

Market Size & Growth

- UAE's generic drugs market is valued at USD 5.02–5.43 billion in 2024, forecast to reach USD 7.24 billion by 2030 (CAGR 6.25–7.7%).
- Generics dominate retail by volume due to government efforts to reduce healthcare costs, manage chronic diseases (notably diabetes: 12.3% adult prevalence), and expand insurance coverage.

Market Structure

- Over 1,200 pharmacies in Dubai alone with rapid growth nationwide; Life Pharmacy has the largest footprint (450+ outlets), followed by Aster, BinSina, Boots, Supercare, Medicina, and others.
- Pharmacy retail chains increasingly offering comprehensive health, wellness, OTC, and e-pharmacy services; Dubai and Abu Dhabi lead in pharmacy density and network expansion.

eCommerce and Digital Health

- E-pharmacy and telemedicine platforms are expanding, providing online prescriptions, home delivery, appointment booking, and medication reminders.
- The Unified Electronic Platform (established by the Ministry of Health and Abu Dhabi DoH) manages electronic prescribing, dispensing, and tracking, focusing especially on controlled and narcotic medicines; real-time regulation and claims.
- WhatsApp and app-based refills now widely accepted, especially in large chains.

OTC Segment & Consumer Trends

- OTC generics, supplements, vitamins, and health/wellness products are fast-growing; front-of-store increasingly diversified to meet health-conscious and affluent expat demand.
- Pharmacy chains also supply medical equipment, beauty, and lifestyle products; bundled chronic care and counseling services are growing.

Market Dynamics

- Rapid urbanization, digital health adoption, policy support, and health tourism contribute to steady retail growth.
- Imports are high for patented medicines and APIs; generics manufacturing promoted through local investment and regulatory support.

Regulatory Environment

- Ministry of Health & Prevention (MOHAP) and local health authorities (Dubai DHA, Abu Dhabi DoH) regulate pricing, reimbursement, and pharmacy standards.
- E-prescription and controlled-substance dispensing via national unified digital platform; insurance compatibility emphasized for access.

Key Challenges & Opportunities

- Affordability, workforce quality, and digital integration are priorities.
- Opportunities in chronic generics, digital/telehealth pharmacy, franchise retail, adherence/support tools, and value-added retail services.

Strategic Considerations

- Integrate e-prescription and telehealth for customer retention.
- Expand high-density chain networks, wellness portfolios, and localized digital retail for a diverse, urbanized UAE population.

China – Pharmaceutical Retail Market Summary (2025)

Market Size & Growth

- China's pharmaceutical market is forecast to achieve revenue exceeding US$125 billion in 2025 with generics forming a significant segment.
- The generic drugs market is expected to grow with a CAGR of ~8.9% (2025–2035) driven by demand for affordable medicines, chronic disease management, and policy support.
- China dominates the global generic API supply chain, controlling ~80% of global production, boosting domestic pharma.

Market Structure

- China had approximately 667,000 pharmacies in 2023, with both chain stores (~58%) and standalone stores contributing to market reach.
- Major pharmacy chains such as Guoda, Dasanlin, Laobaixing, and Yifeng dominate retail pharmacy revenue; chains are growing steadily.
- Online healthcare and e-commerce pharmacies are expanding rapidly, driving shifts in consumer purchasing patterns.

ePrescription and Digital Health

- Electronic prescription adoption in China is fragmented but expanding rapidly with numerous local hospital- and region-based eRx platforms.
- National policies include drug traceability by 2025 mandating real-time scanning of unique drug codes for insurance reimbursement and anti-counterfeit.
- Internet hospitals and electronic prescription services are emerging as key digital health components, especially for outpatient care.

Market Dynamics

- Government initiatives bolster drug traceability, supply chain integrity, and e-prescription uptake, but scale integration remains a challenge.
- Hospital pharmacies are key buyers of specialty and injectables generics, while retail pharmacies serve the mass market.
- Pressure to digitize and modernize combined with rising pharmaceutical exports shapes sector trends.

Consumer Behaviour

- Increasing reliance on e-commerce and digital platforms for medicine purchasing.
- Growing patient access to internet hospitals and digital health tools promotes remote consultation and prescription fulfillment.

Key Drivers

- Government reform agendas, expanding middle-class demand, rising chronic and infectious disease burdens.

Key Challenges

- Fragmented e-prescription regime limits full potential benefits.
- Operational pressures on outpatient pharmacists due to new traceability mandates.

Opportunities for New Entrants

- High-growth specialty generics and biosimilars, e-commerce integrated retail.
- Advanced drug traceability and digital supply chain services.

Regulatory Environment

- National Healthcare Security Administration (NHSA) and State Drug Administration govern pricing, reimbursement, and traceability.
- Continued push for electronic prescriptions with hospital and outpatient integration.

Strategic Considerations

- Invest in digital integration with traceability and internet hospital systems.
- Develop specialty/generic mixes suited to retail and hospital segments.
- Adapt to complex regulatory environment.

Australia – Pharmaceutical Retail Market Summary (2025)

Market Size & Growth

- Generic drug retail value at USD 10.9 billion (2024); projected 5.8% CAGR (2025–33), reaching USD 19.1 billion by 2033.
- Approximately 65% of prescriptions dispensed are generics; value share rising as biosimilars adoption accelerates.

Market Structure

- 5,900+ community pharmacies across the country, with dense urban and regional presence.
- The "Pharmacy Guild network" and banners like Chemist Warehouse, Priceline, and TerryWhite Chemmart dominate.
- Local manufacturing is encouraged by policy; Apotex, Arrow, and Aspen are major generic suppliers.

eCommerce Segment

- E-prescriptions available nationwide since 2020; over 98% of pharmacies are live with digital dispensing.
- Multiple e-prescribing networks (eRx Script Exchange, MediSecure); patients receive QR codes (tokens) for pick-up.
- Telepharmacy and online order/fulfilment options expand, especially for OTC and rural refills.

OTC Segment

- OTC generics and private-label products lead front-of-store sales, especially pain relief, vitamins, allergy, and cold/flu.
- Both in-store and online OTC channels growing as wellness and self-care demand rises.

Market Dynamics

- PBS (Pharmaceutical Benefits Scheme) actively promotes substitution and price parity for generics; pricing set by government with periodic reviews.
- Growing use of biosimilars and complex generics; supply chain bolstered by local investment.

Consumer Behaviour

- High acceptance of generics and pharmacist-led substitution; price transparency and reliability valued.
- Adoption of digital health records, eRx tokens, and home delivery services rising, especially among chronic-care patients.

Key Drivers

- Aging population (17% 65+ in 2024), chronic disease
- PBS expansion
- Government support for manufacturing and digital health.

Key Challenges

- PBS pricing reviews periodically tighten margins; some rural areas face workforce shortages.
- Supply chain vulnerability to global disruptions, but improving.

Opportunities for New Entrants

- Growth niches: biosimilars, complex generics, digital adherence tools, expanded home delivery.
- Partnerships for telepharmacy and regional pharmacy services.

Regulatory Environment

- TGA (Therapeutic Goods Administration) licenses and monitors safety; Department of Health sets PBS terms.
- E-prescribing mandatory for most PBS/RPBS items; pharmacies integrated with national digital dispensing platforms.

Strategic Considerations

- Scale digital workflows
- Optimize inventory for PBS resets
- Leverage private-label growth and telepharmacy to boost reach and margin.

Canada – Pharmaceutical Retail Market Summary (2025)

Market Size & Growth

- Generic drug retail revenue reached USD 10.4 billion in 2024; forecasted 7.3% CAGR (2025–33); accounts for 30–35% of prescription market value and 60–65% by volume.
- Strong growth is supported by high rates of insurance coverage, rising chronic disease prevalence, and ongoing drug cost containment policies.

Market Structure

- 10,432 licensed pharmacies in 2024; major chains include Guardian & IDA (1,422 locations), Shoppers Drug Mart (1,185), and Pharmasave (898).
- Chain stores dominate urban settings; independents more common in rural areas.
- Local manufacturing concentrated among leaders: Apotex, Pharmascience, Sandoz, Mylan, Teva, Sun Pharma.

eCommerce Segment

- National e-prescribing system (PrescribeIT) rolling out, covers partial provinces and expanding; majority of scripts still processed by traditional means.
- Telepharmacy and online refill services are increasing accessibility, especially for remote regions.

OTC Segment

- OTC generics and private-label products account for a significant share of front-of-store sales; pain, cold/flu, vitamins, and allergy categories drive growth.
- Chains promote convenience, price transparency, and online order fulfillment.

Market Dynamics

- Price controls and public formularies incentivize generic substitution; insurance plans and programs favour lower-cost generics for chronic patients.
- High urban pharmacy density, but rural and Indigenous communities still face access challenges.
- Market dynamics driven by regulatory framework, competitive chain consolidation, and digital transformation trends.

Consumer Behaviour

- Canadians show high acceptance of generics, motivated by insurance coverage and pharmacist advice.
- Digital engagement rising: online refills, telepharmacy, and demand for e-prescribing.

Key Drivers

- Aging population (over 19% age 65+ by 2025), persistent chronic illness, and payer cost controls.
- Expanding digital pharmacy infrastructure improves adherence and refills.

Key Challenges

- Rural pharmacy access gaps; supply chain constraints with some generics; uneven eRx rollout.

Opportunities for New Entrants

- Expansion of digital retailing, telepharmacy, and e-prescription integration.
- Private-label and chronic-disease generics in underserved markets.

Regulatory Environment

- Regulator: Health Canada/Provincial Colleges; price policies include reference pricing and substitution mandates.
- PrescribeIT rolling out nationally, connects EMR/EHR with pharmacy systems for secure prescription transfer.

Strategic Considerations

- Scale supply and distribution for large chain networks; expand online access and telepharmacy models across regions; align with payer policies and eRx digital transformation.

Malta – Pharmaceutical Retail Market Summary (2025)

Market Size & Growth

- Retail pharmaceuticals revenue projected around US$172 million in 2025; oncology is the largest therapeutic slice by value among Rx classes.
- OTC retail projected near US$110 million in 2025 with ~5.8% annual growth outlook, reflecting strong self-care demand.

Market Structure

- Over 200 licensed community pharmacies across Malta and Gozo provide high walk-in coverage, with >90% of residents within walking distance of a pharmacy.
- Local manufacturing presence focuses on generics and medicinal gases under Medicines Act licensing.

eCommerce Segment

- ePrescription capability is being integrated within the national CARE system to streamline issuance and dispensing across providers and pharmacies.
- Cross-border prescription distance selling remains constrained under EU safeguards; online services focus on refills, counselling, and compliant local delivery.

OTC Segment

- OTC value is significant relative to Rx due to self-medication, seasonal respiratory, and travel-related demand.
- Online discovery is rising, with purchases fulfilled through community pharmacies under national rules.

Market Dynamics

- Government Formulary List provides free medicines to eligible patients, concentrating value in reimbursed lines while retail private spend covers non-formulary items.
- High physical access and tourist inflows support steady front-of-store turnover and adherence services.
- Price discipline and formulary governance maintain predictable co-pays and encourage substitution in off-patent classes.

Consumer Behaviour

- High trust in community pharmacists for counselling and rapid access, aided by dense pharmacy coverage.
- Eligibility for free formulary medicines steers patient flow through designated pharmacies under the scheme.

Key Drivers

- Universal access mechanisms (Pharmacy of Your Choice) and the Government Formulary List sustain steady prescription volumes.
- Ongoing ePrescription integration improves workflow efficiency and accuracy for prescribers and dispensers.

Key Challenges

- Small national scale limits SKU breadth and bargaining power with multinational suppliers.

Opportunities for New Entrants

- High-rotation generics in chronic classes and travel-related OTC assortments sized to compact demand.
- Service-led offerings: adherence support, quick diagnostics, and tourist-oriented care via dense pharmacy network.
- Partnerships to integrate ePrescription and inventory visibility within CARE-linked workflows.

Regulatory Environment

- Regulator: Malta Medicines Authority oversees authorisation, inspection, and pharmacovigilance.
- ePrescription: integration into CARE aims for streamlined digital prescribing and dispensing across community pharmacies.

Strategic Considerations

- Calibrate pack sizes and range to a compact, tourist-influenced market while ensuring formulary-aligned availability.

Estonia – Pharmaceutical Retail Market Summary (2025)

Market Size & Growth

- Retail pharmaceuticals revenue projected around US$549 million in 2025; generics comprise over 70% of prescriptions by volume.
- Overall market to grow at ~6.6% CAGR 2025–2030, driven by chronic disease prevalence and digitalisation.
- Prescription drugs dominate retail value, with oncology and anti-diabetics leading therapeutic segments.

Market Structure

- Around 500 community pharmacies in 2024, with dense urban coverage and chains like Apotheka leading.
- Fully private ownership; high pharmacist density supports access in a small population.
- Reference pricing caps off-patent SKUs to the lowest EU levels, fostering branded-generic competition.

eCommerce Segment

- ePrescription mandatory since 2010; 100% of prescriptions digital via national system.
- Pharmacies offer online refills and click-and-collect; cross-border Rx shipping limited by EU rules.
- Patients access prescriptions via ID-card or e-Patient Portal for seamless dispensing.

OTC Segment

- OTC sales focus on respiratory, pain, and vitamins; self-medication trends boost private-label generics.
- Online OTC share rising, integrated with eHealth for convenience.
- Compact front-of-store space prioritises high-rotation lines.

Market Dynamics

- Reference pricing and tenders keep generic prices 50–70% below originators.
- Mandatory substitution and pharmacist guidance stabilise high generic penetration.
- Digital infrastructure reduces errors and enables real-time monitoring of adherence.

Consumer Behaviour

- High acceptance of generics due to low co-pays and eHealth transparency.
- Digital refills via e-Patient Portal encourage convenience-oriented purchasing.
- Rural patients benefit from nationwide ePrescription for access without travel.

Key Drivers

- Rising diabetes and oncology needs sustain chronic prescription volumes.
- Full ePrescription digitalisation streamlines workflows and cross-border access.
- Stable demographics with universal insurance underpin predictable demand.

Key Challenges

- Small market scale limits SKU breadth and supplier leverage.
- Occasional shortages in low-priced generics due to EU-wide supply dynamics.
- Continuous eHealth upgrades require pharmacist training.

Opportunities for New Entrants

- High-volume chronic classes like anti-diabetics with steady digital refills.
- Value-added generics and fixed-dose combos in limited-competition niches.
- Adherence tools integrated with ePrescription for chronic management.

Regulatory Environment

- Regulator: State Agency of Medicines oversees authorisation and pharmacovigilance.
- Pricing: reference to lowest EU prices; mandatory substitution for generics.
- ePrescription: compulsory, centralised system with 100% uptake; real-time validation via national portal.

Strategic Considerations

- Align SKUs to reference-price tenders and pack for a compact market.

Slovakia – Pharmaceutical Retail Market Summary (2025)

Market Size & Growth

- Retail pharmacy turnover roughly €1.1 bn in 2024; value trend +6% YoY, units +1%.
- Generics fill about 70% of prescriptions and contribute ≈35% of retail value.
- Retail medicines market projected to advance ~3% CAGR 2025-2027 as chronic-therapy volumes rise.

Market Structure

- 1,929 community-pharmacy businesses in 2024 after post-deregulation doubling.
- Chains Dr. Max and Benu lead; ownership fully private.
- Maximum ex-factory for off-patent SKUs set via external-reference basket (average of lowest three EU prices).

eCommerce Segment

- ePrescription nationwide since 2018; >90% of scripts digital via eHealth portal.
- Pharmacies offer click-and-collect and local courier; cross-border Rx shipping barred.
- Patients use Citizen Health eBook to track repeats and co-pays.

OTC Segment

- Pain, cold, and vitamin lines dominate; private-label generics anchor low-price tier.
- Online OTC value share ≈7% and climbing.
- Front-of-store space prioritises high-rotation SKUs.

Market Dynamics

- Reference-pricing resets and tenders keep generic prices 40–60% below originator.
- Mandatory substitution plus pharmacist counselling stabilise generic unit share.
- Margin compression triggers periodic supply gaps in low-priced SKUs.

Consumer Behaviour

- Universal insurance and low co-pays drive high generic acceptance.
- Digital refills and price transparency via eHealth foster convenience.
- Cross-border commuters sometimes fill OTCs in neighbouring Austria/Czechia for selection.

Key Drivers

- Ageing population and high cardio-metabolic burden sustain script growth.
- Government cost-containment anchors generic substitution.
- Mature eHealth infrastructure streamlines prescribing–dispensing cycle.

Key Challenges

- Tight price caps erode profitability for older generics.
- Occasional stock-outs tied to low EU-benchmark prices and export.
- Rural pharmacist shortages persist.

Opportunities for New Entrants

- High-volume chronic drugs (statins, PPIs, ACEIs) frequently retendered.
- Fixed-dose combos and value-added generics in niches with limited competition.
- Adherence apps and dose-dispensing services linked to ePrescription.

Regulatory Environment

- Regulator: State Institute for Drug Control (ŠÚKL) licenses products and pharmacies.
- Pricing: external reference to three lowest EU prices; mandatory 45% discount at LOE; annual tenders for high-volume lines.
- ePrescription: compulsory, integrated with national eHealth and insurers; real-time claim validation.

Strategic Considerations

- Align pack sizes and bid cycles to reference-price resets; safeguard supply amid low margins.
- Invest in digital services and loyalty programmes within eHealth ecosystem.
- Balance ethical–generic mix and expand OTC private-label to offset margin squeeze.

Hungary – Pharmaceutical Retail Market Summary (2025)

Market Size & Growth

- Generics account for roughly two-thirds of outpatient scripts but just over one-quarter of spending (2023).
- Retail pharmacy turnover is expected to rise at about 4% CAGR in 2023-2027.
- Statin reimbursement dropped 63% between 2010-2019 after successive price cuts.

Market Structure

- 2,260 community pharmacies in 2023, including 613 branches and 142 GP-run rural units.
- All privately owned; most join regional buying groups while keeping individual licences.
- Monthly reference-price clusters set by the National Health Insurance Fund guide dispensing.

eCommerce Segment

- Mandatory e-Prescription (EESZT) since 2018; >95% of scripts filled paper-free.
- Verified pharmacies offer click-and-collect or courier delivery; cross-border Rx sales barred.
- Patients use national e-ID to view repeats, co-pays, and stock in the EESZT portal.

OTC Segment

- Selected OTC analgesics, cold remedies, GI products, vitamins sold in supermarket drugstore corners; higher-risk items remain pharmacy-only.
- Private-label generics expanding, especially in pain and allergy.
- Seasonal respiratory/allergy peaks can generate one-third of annual OTC turnover.

Market Dynamics

- Blind-bidding resets prices quarterly, each generic undercutting the current lowest.
- Mandatory generic prescribing for statins, PPIs steers demand to the cheapest reimbursed pack.
- Regressive wholesale-retail margins squeeze profits as ex-factory prices fall.

Consumer Behaviour

- High trust in generics reinforced by EU bioequivalence and pharmacist counselling.
- Wide EESZT app adoption supports refills, price checks, and adherence.
- Price-sensitive households split Rx and eligible OTC purchases across channels.

Key Drivers

- Budget caps and reference pricing sustain generic penetration while limiting payer spend.
- One-fifth of the population is ≥65 years, boosting chronic cardiovascular and metabolic volumes.
- Full e-Prescription coverage enables scalable digital adherence services.

Key Challenges

- Thin margins threaten viability of rural pharmacies.
- Post-tender stockouts occur as manufacturers adjust to lower prices.
- Ongoing pharmacist out-migration to higher-wage EU markets.

Opportunities for New Entrants

- High-volume chronic therapies in frequently retendered clusters (statins, ACE inhibitors, PPIs).
- Dose-dispensing and adherence programs integrated with EESZT.
- Private-label OTC generics tailored for supermarket drugstore corners.

Regulatory Environment

- Regulator: National Centre for Public Health and Pharmacy licences pharmacies and monitors GMP.
- Pricing/Reimbursement: National Health Insurance Fund runs blind bidding, sets reference prices, applies regressive margins.

Strategic Considerations

- Optimise pack sizes and bids to retain top-tier reimbursement status.
- Use analytics to balance inventory around quarterly price resets and prevent stockouts.

Luxembourg – Pharmaceutical Retail Market Summary (2025)

Market Size & Growth

- Retail pharmacy turnover ≈ €270 m (MAT Feb-2025); total value +5% YoY, generic/copy value +1%, units flat.
- Retail pharma revenue projected ≈ US$287 m for 2025; generic value growth trails market under sustained price pressure.

Market Structure

- IQVIA sell-in splits ethical vs. unbranded generics for all community-pharmacy sales.
- Small population and cross-border care limit volume and SKU depth.
- Buying groups and distributors set generic prices and supply terms.

eCommerce Segment

- Provider e-invoicing starts 2026; national e-prescription to follow, connecting prescribers and pharmacies.
- Digital claims already paper-free; Rx distance selling remains restricted.
- Online services focus on click-and-collect, counselling, local delivery.

OTC Segment

- Pharmacies lead; respiratory/allergy peaks dominate seasonality.
- Private-label generics anchor low-price tier; limited shelf space targets high-rotation lines.

Market Dynamics

- Ethical brands drive most value growth; generics keep unit share but face price compression.
- Compact logistics and negotiated discounts shape shelf pricing and availability.

Consumer Behaviour

- Universal insurance and high incomes favour substitution when copay savings are clear.
- Digital claim flows foster expectation of paper-free refills; e-Rx will reinforce this trend.

Key Drivers

- Chronic cardiovascular, metabolic, and CNS needs sustain prescription volume.
- Policy digitalisation promises leaner prescribing-dispensing cycles.
- Stable demographics with broad coverage support steady demand.

Key Challenges

- Price pressure slows generic value growth.
- Small market heightens sensitivity to supply interruptions.
- Coordinated IT upgrades needed for forthcoming e-prescription.

Opportunities for New Entrants

- Supply high-rotation chronic therapies with reliable pricing.
- Embed adherence and refill services into the upcoming e-Rx workflow.
- Develop value-led private-label OTC lines.

Regulatory Environment

- Pharmacies licensed by national health authority; reimbursement via positive list and third-party payment.
- E-invoicing 2026, e-prescription thereafter; Rx distance selling still limited.
- Generic entry typically 40–70% below originator list price.

Strategic Considerations

- Fine-tune pack sizes and prices to defend unit share amid tight margins.
- Upgrade systems for e-Rx and insurer-app connectivity.
- Balance ethical and generic mix to safeguard profit while keeping therapies affordable.

Romania – Pharmaceutical Retail Market Summary (2025)

Market Size & Growth

- Retail pharmacy turnover RON 18.5 bn (€3.7 bn) MAT Jun-2025; value +11%, units +1%.
- Generics ≈ 67% of scripts and ≈ 30% of value; retail market projected to expand ~4% CAGR 2025-2027 despite price caps.

Market Structure

- 8,247 community pharmacies in 2023; Dr. Max 941 and Catena 929 outlets lead.
- Entirely private ownership; dense urban, sparse rural coverage.
- Off-patent prices fixed at the lowest of a 12-EU-country basket.

eCommerce Segment

- National e-Prescription live since 2012; >90% of scripts electronic.
- Pharmacies may courier locally; cross-border Rx shipping barred.
- Health-card portal lets patients view co-pays and repeats.

OTC Segment

- Self-medication lifts respiratory, pain, vitamin sales; seasonal peaks drive one-third of turnover.
- Online OTC <5% of value but rising; chains push private-label generics.
- Limited shelf space favours high-rotation lines.

Market Dynamics

- Claw-back tax (15% generics, 25% branded) plus periodic price cuts squeeze margins.
- EU-low prices fuel parallel export and spot shortages.
- Cost-volume contracts cap spend on high-budget therapies.

Consumer Behaviour

- Generics widely accepted via low co-pays and pharmacist advice.
- Price-sensitive shoppers split: Rx in-store, OTC online.
- Rural patients rely on courier or periodic urban trips.

Key Drivers

- Ageing population (≈ 20% ≥65 yrs) and high cardio-metabolic burden sustain volumes.
- Rising incomes boost OTC and supplement spend.
- Digital infrastructure (e-Rx, health card) streamlines refills and adherence.

Key Challenges

- Profit erosion from claw-back and reference pricing.
- Supply volatility from parallel trade and manufacturer exits.
- Pharmacist shortages outside cities.

Opportunities for New Entrants

- High-volume chronic classes: statins, PPIs, ACEIs.
- Fixed-dose combos and value-added generics in limited-competition niches.
- E-Rx-linked adherence apps and blister packs for chronic users.

Regulatory Environment

- Regulator: National Agency for Medicines and Medical Devices.
- Pricing: lowest-basket reference plus mandatory 35% discount at patent expiry; claw-back updated quarterly.
- e-Prescription platform links prescribers, pharmacies, insurers with real-time validation.

Strategic Considerations

- Configure SKUs and logistics for low price ceilings and claw-back impact.
- Secure steady supply to avoid shortages and gain chain preference.
- Add clinical and digital services to offset squeezed generic margins.

USA – Pharmaceutical Retail Market Summary (2025)

Market Size & Growth

- Generics+biosimilars filled 90% of prescriptions and accounted for 13.1% of prescription drug spending (2023)
- Average generic copay $7.05 vs. brand $27.10 (2023)
- Pharmaceuticals' share of health spending is tracked in OECD series for cross-country context; retail generics are not separately valued by OECD

Market Structure

- Nationwide geographic analysis documents community pharmacy access and distribution across the U.S. (2022)
- Retail dispensing through chain and independent pharmacies under state licensure; participation in PBM networks determines reimbursement and channel access
- Generics dominate retail volume; state substitution laws and payer formularies guide pharmacy-level dispensing

eCommerce Segment

- Licensed mail-order and online pharmacy channels operate under federal/state rules and integrate with electronic prescribing for remote fulfillment
- E-prescribing widely adopted in outpatient care with standardized electronic transmission supporting retail and mail-order workflows
- Retail pharmacies provide online refills, home delivery, and auto-refill programs linked to e-prescriptions

OTC Segment

- Generic OTCs widely sold via pharmacies, supermarkets, and mass retail; key categories include analgesics, cough/cold, gastrointestinal, and allergy
- Store-brand generics drive price-sensitive OTC purchasing; seasonal demand (respiratory/allergy) shapes turnover
- Pharmacy counseling and immunization services reinforce self-care purchasing in retail settings

Market Dynamics

- PBM formularies and tiered benefits steer dispensing to lowest-net-cost generics; patient cost-share varies by plan design
- High generic utilization reflects automatic substitution under state laws and payer incentives

Consumer Behaviour

- High acceptance of generics driven by low copays and broad coverage; generics fill most retail prescriptions
- Loss of exclusivity and a steady ANDA pipeline sustain generic entry across therapeutic areas

Key Challenges

- Margin compression from fees/chargebacks and reimbursement dynamics within PBM contracts

Opportunities for New Entrants

- Limited-competition generics and complex dosage forms where supply is constrained
- Adherence and synchronized refill programs with plans/providers leveraging e-prescribing

Regulatory Environment

- Regulator: U.S. Food and Drug Administration oversees ANDA approvals, bioequivalence, and GMP compliance
- ePrescription/EPS: Electronic prescribing widely used with national standards supporting outpatient transmission and controlled substances workflows

Strategic Considerations

- Prioritize high-volume chronic therapies and limited-competition segments to balance price pressure and supply reliability
- Deepen PBM/payer engagement for formulary positioning and preferred networks; invest in adherence services to improve persistence.

Czech Republic – Pharmaceutical Retail Market (2025)

Market Size & Growth

- Broader pharmaceuticals market projected USD 5.38bn (2025), 6.25% CAGR to USD 7.28bn by 2030
- Pharmacy retail market projected US$5.10bn (2025), 3.66% CAGR 2025-2029
- Generic medicines constitute >30% of total pharmaceutical market share

Market Structure

- Several pharmacy chains hold majority market share with hundreds of independent pharmacies
- Prague expected to dominate due to pharmaceutical company concentration
- Generic share estimated ≈60% of prescription drug market within retail sector

eCommerce Segment

- European ePharmacy market context: USD 22.66bn (2025) with 15.1% CAGR to USD 69.8bn by 2033
- Online pharmacies included in distribution channel segmentation

OTC Segment

- OTC drugs included in broader pharmaceutical market segmentation
- OTC segment part of drug type classification alongside prescription drugs

Market Dynamics

- Original brand must reduce price by 30% three months after first generic enters market
- Generic substitution effectively reduces pharmaceutical expenditures
- Share of generics accounted for 34.4% of volume (2011), below OECD-19 average of 40.5%
- Branded drugs segment expected fastest growth driven by chronic disease demand

Consumer Behaviour

- Growing demand for innovative, high-value pharmaceuticals driven by chronic disease burden
- Patient preferences influenced by government reimbursement coverage and accessibility
- Cost savings and affordability driving generic adoption

Key Drivers

- Rising healthcare expenditure and government spending on healthcare
- Increasing chronic disease prevalence: 791.4k diabetes patients (2021) rising to 799.2k by 2030
- Cancer prevalence >700k with ≈60k new cases annually
- Government reimbursement programs improving medication accessibility

Key Challenges

- Heavily regulated environment with strict import/export controls
- Intense price competition and thin profit margins in generic segment
- Price regulations and stringent regulatory approvals impacting profitability
- Generic competition affecting branded pharmaceutical returns

Opportunities for New Entrants

- Anti-diabetic segment expansion with increasing diabetes prevalence
- Growing demand for cost-effective treatments amid rising healthcare costs
- Digital health technologies and personalized medicine adoption trends
- Expanding reimbursement coverage for new and innovative drugs

Regulatory Environment

- SÚKL (State Institute for Drug Control) serves as primary regulatory authority
- Ministry of Health oversight with Strategic Plan 2021-2025 framework
- EU regulatory alignment supporting generic substitution policies

Strategic Considerations

- Generic medicines >30% market share indicates moderate acceptance with growth potential
- Prague-centric market concentration offers strategic positioning opportunities

Germany – Pharmaceutical Retail Market Summary (2025)

Market Size & Growth

- Broader Pharmaceutical Market size USD 68.82 billion (2025), CAGR 6.20% to USD 92.97 billion by 2030
- Generic Drugs Market valued USD 35.13 billion (2024), projected USD 55.16 billion by 2032, CAGR 5.8%
- Retail Pharmacy Market projected USD 94,608.74 million (2024) to USD 134,510.85 million by 2032, CAGR 4.50%

Market Structure

- 16,803 pharmacies operating as of mid-2025, decrease of 238 from end-2024 (17,041)
- Pharmacy density 21 per 100,000 inhabitants
- Generic medicines share 80% by volume in retail sector

eCommerce Segment

- OTC Drugs eCommerce market projected US$2,164.0 million by 2025
- Accounts for 95.7% of total Pharmaceuticals eCommerce market

OTC Segment

- OTC drug market USD 9.50 billion (2025), projected USD 11.68 billion by 2030, CAGR 4.23%
- OTC Pharmaceuticals revenue US$10.68 billion by 2025, CAGR 2.56% to US$11.81 billion by 2029
- Self-medication trend drives 40.2% adult prevalence

Market Dynamics

- Prompt payment cash discounts up to 3% allowed on Rx medicinal products from 2025
- Generic substitution mandatory for pharmacists unless medically justified
- Retail segment dominates with 80% generic volume share
- E-prescriptions mandatory for OTC extension in 2025

Consumer Behaviour

- 40.2% adults engage in self-medication, higher among women (47.2%)
- Increasing preference for preventive care and natural alternatives
- Digital health adoption drives online purchases for convenience

Key Drivers

- Ageing population and chronic disease prevalence fuel demand
- Healthcare budget supports cost-effective generic promotion
- E-pharmacy expansion through digital prescriptions

Key Challenges

- Pharmacy closures at 238 in first half 2025 due to economic pressures
- 25% pharmacies earning below €75,000 annually

Opportunities for New Entrants

- Patent expirations open generic market potential
- E-pharmacy growth with 16.38% online revenue share by 2025
- High generic acceptance (80% volume) in retail sector

Regulatory Environment

- BfArM regulates with focus on digital health data access from 2025
- Medical Research Act enables confidential reimbursement pricing
- Gets challenging to find verified data available from Germany Ministry of Health on specific retail pharmacy regulatory frameworks

Strategic Considerations

- Mandatory generic substitution supports retail cost efficiency
- Digital patient records enhance self-medication trends
- Pharmacy density decline creates consolidation opportunities

Switzerland – Pharmaceutical Retail Market Summary (2025)

Market Size & Growth

- While no verified data is available for specific generic pharmaceutical retail market size, Broader pharmaceuticals market is projected to be US$7.29bn (2025)
- Generic medicines market share 25.2% by volume (2025 projection)
- Overall pharmaceutical market expected 3.80% CAGR 2025-2034

Market Structure

- 1,773 retail pharmacies operating nationwide (as of 2024)
- Generic substitution rate averaged 77.3% in major pharmacy networks (April 2025)
- Independent pharmacies dominate with limited chain concentration
- No verified data available for specific generic vs branded retail market share breakdown

eCommerce Segment

- Online pharmacy market experiencing strong growth with digital adoption
- Major chains reporting double-digit online sales increases (2025)
- Digital prescription systems supporting online fulfillment expansion

OTC Segment

- OTC pharmaceuticals market projected US$1.87bn (2025), 3.38% CAGR 2025-2029
- Largest segment "Other OTC Pharmaceuticals" at US$461.71m (2025)
- Consumer shift toward self-medication and preventive products driving demand
- Pharmacy healthcare services grew 13% with >95,000 consultations (first four months 2025)

Market Dynamics

- Mandatory 30% price reduction for original brands three months after first generic entry
- High demand for GLP-1 weight loss medications boosting retail sales since 2024
- Seasonal flu outbreaks (Q1 2025) increased prescription volumes significantly
- Competitive pressure in consumer healthcare with 1.8% market growth

Consumer Behaviour

- Strong preference for convenient access via digital and in-store channels
- Growing demand for natural, herbal, and preventive healthcare remedies
- High health consciousness promoting self-care and wellness products
- Increasing use of pharmacy advisory services for generic recommendations

Key Drivers

- Aging population and rising chronic disease prevalence sustaining demand
- High disposable income and stable economy enabling retail access
- Digital transformation accelerating ePharmacy and service integration
- Government policies promoting cost-effective generic substitution

Key Challenges

- Supply chain dependencies creating vulnerability to global disruptions
- Price pressure from mandatory reductions post-generic entry
- Competition from emerging digital-first pharmacy models

Opportunities for New Entrants

- Expanding OTC segment with 3.38% annual growth projection
- Integration of digital health and telemedicine in retail settings
- Partnerships for healthcare service expansion in pharmacies

Regulatory Environment

- Federal Office of Public Health (FOPH) oversees pharmaceutical regulations
- Mandatory generic substitution encouraged for cost control

Strategic Considerations

- High substitution rates (77.3%) support generic market penetration
- Digital integration essential for competing in eCommerce growth

Mozambique – Pharmaceutical Retail Market Summary (2025)

Market Size & Growth

- Broader Pharmacies market projected US$163.89 million by 2025
- No verified data available for specific generic pharmaceutical retail market size in Mozambique for 2025
- Africa generic pharmaceutical market USD 6.43 billion in 2022, 4.32% CAGR 2023-2030

Market Structure

- 293 pharmacies operating as of 2012, 60% concentrated in Maputo
- Pharmaceutical access increased from 10% (1975) to 80% (2007)
- Registered products reduced from 26,000 to 1,200 since independence
- No verified data available for generic versus branded market share

eCommerce Segment

- Internet penetration 20.7% with 6.92 million users January 2023
- Mobile money solutions M-PESA, mKesh, e-Mola used for transactions
- No verified data available for ePharmacy market size or penetration rates

OTC Segment

- OTC market generated US$59.94 million revenue in 2025
- Expected 7.63% annual growth (CAGR 2025-2029)
- Customer preferences shift towards self-medication and herbal remedies

Market Dynamics

- Parliament ended Medimoc monopoly through "controlled liberalization"
- Many pharmacies sell prescription drugs without prescription despite restrictions
- Growing multinational pharmaceutical company presence

Consumer Behaviour

- Shift towards self-medication avoiding doctor visits for minor ailments
- Growing preference for herbal remedies perceived as safer
- High malaria prevalence drives OTC prevention/treatment demand

Key Drivers

- Population growth, urbanization, increasing disposable income
- High infectious disease burden and limited rural healthcare access
- E-commerce platforms and mobile payment solutions expansion

Key Challenges

- Limited credit/debit card access restricts online purchases
- Underdeveloped infrastructure creates e-commerce barriers
- No verified data available for supply chain challenges

Opportunities for New Entrants

- Large underserved rural population
- Post-Medimoc monopoly market opportunities
- Growing middle class and mobile payment adoption

Regulatory Environment

- Resolution 18/2025 establishes new licensing framework
- ANARME serves as regulatory authority
- Companies require medically-qualified technical director and wholesale operations
- No verified data available from Mozambique Ministry of Health on specific retail frameworks

Strategic Considerations

- New competitive environment post-monopoly
- Limited internet but mobile payment alternatives available
- Geographic expansion opportunities beyond Maputo concentration
- Regulations allow pharmaceutical vending machines.

Belgium – Pharmaceutical Retail Market Summary (2025)

Market Size & Growth

- Broader pharmaceuticals market projected US$5.80bn (2025)
- Prescription drugs segment projected US$7.17bn (2025), 3.29% CAGR 2025-2029
- Overall pharmacies market projected US$8.41bn (2025), 5.87% CAGR to US$11.17bn by 2030

Market Structure

- Approximately 5,800 retail pharmacies and parapharmacies operating nationwide
- Independent pharmacies dominate with 85% market share; chains hold remaining 15%
- Generic medicines share around 80% by volume in retail sector
- Pharmacy density high with focus on accessible community-based retail operations

eCommerce Segment

- Online pharmacy market generated US$295m (2024), projected 10-15% growth into 2025
- ePharmacy platforms handle OTC and repeat prescriptions with high digital adoption

OTC Segment

- OTC pharmaceuticals market revenue projected US$1.24bn (2025), 2.83% CAGR 2025-2029
- Other OTC segment (non-core) projected US$245.90m (2025)
- Growing self-medication trends drive retail OTC generic demand

Market Dynamics

- Generic substitution mandatory for reimbursable prescriptions unless opted out
- Retail market shows 0.6% value growth; generics/copies up 0.3% (MAT April 2025)
- Monthly price adjustments via national tariff system pressure retail margins
- High competition among independents and emerging chains in urban areas

Consumer Behaviour

- Strong preference for affordable generics due to compulsory insurance coverage
- Increasing self-care and digital ordering for convenience in retail purchases
- High trust in community pharmacies for generic advice and accessibility

Key Drivers

- Rising chronic disease burden and aging population boost retail generic demand
- Healthcare spending at 11% GDP supports pharmaceutical access
- Digital infrastructure expansion enables ePharmacy growth

Key Challenges

- Supply chain volatility from global dependencies affects retail availability
- Narrow margins from reimbursement caps and price controls

Opportunities for New Entrants

- Expansion in ePharmacy with automated repeat dispensing models
- Growing OTC generics in parapharmacies and online channels
- Urban retail formats leveraging high pharmacy density

Regulatory Environment

- Federal Agency for Medicines and Health Products (FAMHP) oversees retail licensing
- Reimbursement via national health insurance promotes generic use

Strategic Considerations

- Mandatory substitution favors cost-effective generics in retail
- Digital integration key for competing in eCommerce segment
- Independent dominance suggests partnerships for chain expansion
- Focus on chronic care generics aligns with demographic trends

United Kingdom – Pharmaceutical Retail Market Summary (2025)

Market Size & Growth

- Total pharmaceutical market projected ≈£36.1 bn (≈US$45.9 bn) by 2025
- Retail-pharmacy revenue £15.3 bn (2023) with 1.8 – 2.2% CAGR to 2029
- Generics ≥80% of prescriptions but only 32 – 35% of value dispensed
- No verified institutional figure for 2025 retail-generic market value

Market Structure

- >11,400 community pharmacies under NHS/PSNC frameworks
- Standard national contract governs reimbursement for NHS scripts
- Generics supplied via Drug Tariff; majority imported from India & EU
- Local manufacturing limited; UK largely reliant on overseas APIs

eCommerce Segment

- ePharmacy fully legal; widely used for repeat NHS prescriptions
- >2.5 m patients enrolled in electronic repeat dispensing (eRD, 2023)
- Certified platforms (e.g., Pharmacy2U, LloydsDirect) process Rx & OTC
- Penetration estimated 10 – 12% of retail volume and rising

OTC Segment

- OTC market projected >£3.1 bn (2025)
- Core categories: pain, allergy, GI, cold/flu
- Supermarkets and online channels expanding OTC generic share
- NHS self-care campaigns boost non-prescription demand

Market Dynamics

- Generic substitution incentivised but not legally mandatory
- Monthly Drug Tariff adjusts reimbursement prices, tightening margins
- High generic usage driven by NHS cost containment policies
- Market remains highly regulated and margin-sensitive

Consumer Behaviour

- Strong trust in NHS-approved generics; efficacy viewed as equivalent
- Rapid uptake of pharmacy apps for scripts & OTC ordering
- Price sensitivity moderate: capped co-pays in England; none in devolved nations
- OTC alternatives preferred for minor ailments to ease GP workload

Key Drivers

- NHS cost-containment measures favour generics
- Rising chronic disease prevalence (diabetes, CVD, asthma)
- Ageing population with multimorbidity requires long-term therapy
- Expanding digital infrastructure and EPS adoption

Key Challenges

- Brexit-related supply volatility for some molecules
- Narrow pharmacy profit margins under fixed Drug Tariff caps
- Regulatory complexity with monthly price revisions
- No nationwide mandate for automatic substitution

Opportunities for New Entrants

- High-volume generics aligned to stable NHS demand areas
- Tech-integrated ePharmacy services (delivery, auto-refills)
- Private OTC generics and supplement-adjacent products
- Urban micro-pharmacies offering rapid access and advice

Regulatory Environment

- MHRA oversees licensing; NHS England sets reimbursement
- Community Pharmacy Contractual Framework governs payments & services

Strategic Considerations

- Align portfolios with Drug Tariff tiers and prescribing trends
- Invest in EPS-linked repeat-delivery models
- Leverage OTC generics via pharmacy chains & supermarkets
- Monitor MHRA post-Brexit regulatory shifts for supply resilience

Netherlands – Pharmaceutical Retail Market Summary (2025)

Market Size & Growth

- The broader Pharmaceuticals market in Netherlands is expected to reach US$6.28 billion in revenue for 2025
- The Prescription Drugs market in Netherlands is projected to reach US$5.54 billion in revenue for 2025

Market Structure

- 1,953 public pharmacies operating in Netherlands as of January 2024
- Generic pharmaceuticals accounted for 81.4% of reimbursed volumes in 2023
- Average medicine costs per pharmacy approximately 1.5 million euros per pharmacy in 2018

eCommerce Segment

- The broader Europe ePharmacy market is estimated at USD 22.66 billion in 2025 growing at 15.1% CAGR

OTC Segment

- The OTC Pharmaceuticals market in Netherlands generated revenue of US$1.15 billion in 2025
- Expected to grow annually by 3.17% (CAGR 2025-2029) for OTC segment
- Customer preferences are shifting towards self-care and self-medication
- Growing popularity of preventive healthcare and management of long-term conditions

Market Dynamics

- Generic substitution occurred at 25% of branded prescriptions according to pharmacy database analysis
- Individually owned pharmacies had lower probability of generic substitution compared to chain pharmacies
- Branded substitution occurred in 10% of generic prescriptions

Consumer Behaviour

- Dutch population places high value on accessible and affordable healthcare including pharmaceuticals
- Patients are generally well-informed and actively involved in healthcare decisions leading to demand for personalized medicine
- Shift towards health and wellness products influenced by increased disposable income and health consciousness
- Generic substitution more likely to occur to patients that were older and more experienced in drug use

Key Drivers

- Government's increased healthcare budget which has risen by 7.2%
- Reduction in inflation from 4.1% in December 2024 to 3.3% in January 2025 coupled with 4.5% increase in wages
- Government focus on affordability and accessibility driving continued generic pharmaceutical use
- Aging population and increasing prevalence of chronic diseases

Opportunities for New Entrants

- Strong preference for cost-effective healthcare solutions with 81.4% generic share of reimbursed volumes
- Stable economic conditions and improved consumer purchasing power creating favorable environment
- Well-developed healthcare system emphasizing patient empowerment and self-management

Regulatory Environment

- Medicines Evaluation Board (CBG) issues marketing authorisation for Dutch market
- Marketing authorisation valid for 5 years with renewal consideration by CBG
- Manufacturers must comply with Maximum Prices for Medicines Regulation

Strategic Considerations

- Generic pharmaceuticals accounting for 81.4% of reimbursed volumes indicates strong market acceptance
- Individual pharmacies versus chain pharmacies show different substitution patterns creating strategic considerations

Sweden – Pharmaceutical Retail Market Summary (2025)

Market Size & Growth

- Total pharmaceutical market (2023): SEK 53.7B (~$5.2B USD).
- Generics represent approximately 62% of prescription volume and 29–32% of retail value by reimbursement cost.
- Generic substitution is mandatory for all reimbursed prescriptions unless clinically exempted.
- Estimated CAGR (2025–2029): 2.3–2.7%, driven by chronic therapy expansion and aging population.
- Per capita pharmaceutical spending: ~$480 USD, with 85% subsidized through the national health system.

Market Structure

- Sweden has around 1,400 licensed community pharmacies operating under strict regulation.
- Reimbursement and pricing systems are standardized nationwide via TLV and Läkemedelsverket.
- A monthly bidding system determines eligible generics for substitution and reimbursement.
- Most generics are imported from the EU and India, as domestic production is limited.

eCommerce Segment

- More than 60% of adults have used ePharmacy services, mostly for prescription refills and wellness products.
- ePharmacy platforms must be integrated with the national ePrescription registry.
- ePharmacy accounts for 15–18% of retail pharmacy sales, with an expected CAGR of 7%.

OTC Segment

- OTC accounts for 15–20% of pharmacy sales by volume.
- Supermarkets are allowed to sell low-risk OTC drugs, subject to classification rules.
- Pharmacists influence OTC decisions, especially for dual-status molecules.

Market Dynamics

- Universal e-prescription infrastructure supports substitution and tracking.
- Substitution compliance exceeds 95% nationwide.

Consumer Behaviour

- Strong public trust in generics due to system transparency and safety standards.
- Low out-of-pocket spending, protected by annual co-pay ceilings.
- Digital tools are widely used for managing chronic therapies and purchasing OTCs.

Key Drivers

- National budget pressure to control drug costs.
- Mandatory monthly substitution model.
- Rising burden of chronic illnesses such as cardiovascular disease and diabetes.
- Full integration of eHealth and prescription systems.

Key Challenges

- Margin compression for pharmacies due to fixed price limits.
- Monthly reimbursement price changes complicate forecasting.
- Limited local manufacturing increases reliance on EU and Asia supply chains.
- Regulatory complexity for serialization and EU compliance.

Opportunities

- Chronic refill generics can be offered through subscription models.
- Retail chains may develop private-label generics for common therapies.
- AI-enabled platforms can bundle adherence services with generics.
- Governed by Läkemedelsverket, TLV, and the Swedish eHealth Agency.
- Generics must comply with monthly pricing adjustments to qualify for reimbursement.

Strategic Considerations

- Register products in the TLV generic substitution schedule.
- Focus on stable-demand categories such as diabetes and heart health.

Ireland – Pharmaceutical Retail Market Summary (2025)

Market Size & Growth

- Total pharmaceutical expenditure (2023): ~€2.3B, including public and private spend
- Generics account for ~75% of prescription volume, but only ~36–40% of market value
- CAGR (2025–2029): ~2.8%, influenced by demographic trends and biosimilar entry

Market Structure

- ~1,900 community pharmacies, mostly independently owned
- Dominant wholesalers: Uniphar, United Drug, PCO
- Major retail chains: LloydsPharmacy Ireland, Hickey's Pharmacy, Boots Ireland
- Local manufacturers of generics are limited; imports dominate (UK, Germany, India)

eCommerce Segment

- ePharmacy for OTC products is legal through certified pharmacies
- Rx medicines must be dispensed in person, with no online fulfillment permitted
- Certified online platforms: Boots.ie (OTC only), LloydsPharmacy.ie
- eCommerce growth is limited by infrastructure and policy constraints

OTC Segment

- OTC market share estimated at ~€480–520M, including both branded and generics
- Common OTC generics: pain relief, flu, digestive health, dermatology, vitamins

Market Dynamics

- INN prescribing is encouraged under the Health (Pricing and Supply of Medical Goods) Act
- Generic substitution by pharmacists is mandatory unless "do not substitute" is specified
- The HSE reimbursement scheme lists generics and reference pricing tiers

Consumer Behaviour

- High public trust in HPRA-approved generics
- Price sensitivity exists for OTCs and non-reimbursed prescriptions
- Pharmacist guidance is a key influencer in substitution and product selection

Key Drivers

- Aging population (>20% aged 65+ by 2025)
- Chronic disease prevalence (diabetes, hypertension, depression)
- Expansion of biosimilar and high-value generics in retail market

Key Challenges

- High import dependency increases exposure to supply shocks
- Reimbursement delays and approval lags from HSE can limit access
- No central ePharmacy model for Rx refills or chronic medication adherence

Opportunities

- Chronic condition bundles via retail + OTC generics
- Private-label OTC generics under chain brands
- National digital health expansion may support future ePharmacy legislation

Regulatory Environment

- Regulated by:
- HPRA (Health Products Regulatory Authority)
- HSE (Health Service Executive)
- Department of Health (gov.ie)
- Generic substitution legally enabled and widely practiced
- OTC sales online are permitted only by registered pharmacy websites

Strategic Considerations

- Position within HSE-reimbursed generic groups
- Leverage pharmacist-driven models for substitution + chronic therapy
- Partner with major pharmacy chains for urban retail scale + digital expansion

Belarus – Pharmaceutical Retail Market Summary (2025)

Market Size & Growth

- Total pharmaceutical market (2022): BYN 3.5B ($1.3B USD equivalent).
- Generics represent ~70–75% of prescription volume, ~40–45% of value in the retail channel.
- Retail generics dominate outpatient care due to pricing mandates and local production scale.
- Pharmaceutical expenditure per capita: ~$140 (2022).
- CAGR (2025–2029): No official forecast; retail generics projected to grow modestly with chronic disease burden and state substitution policies.

Market Structure

- ~3,500 licensed pharmacies, with a public–private mix dominated by state-aligned distribution.
- State-regulated pricing and procurement systems shape retail access and inventory.
- Private pharmacies operate under uniform pricing controls, reducing brand competition.
- Local manufacturers supply 50–60% of domestic needs; retail market depends on stable import channels for APIs and specialized formulations.

eCommerce Segment

- ePharmacy is allowed for OTC products only; no online sale or delivery of prescription drugs is permitted.
- Only pharmacies licensed through national regulators may operate digital storefronts.
- Urban ePharmacy usage is emerging, especially for supplements and wellness products, but remains <2% of total pharmacy retail volume.
- No official value estimate is available for the eCommerce segment in 2025.

OTC Segment

- Major OTC generic categories include pain relief, cold/flu, GI health, topical treatments, and basic supplements.
- Vitamins (especially C and D), paracetamol, and rehydration salts are widely sold over the counter.

Market Dynamics

- Essential Medicines List and INN prescribing dominate the public sector and influence retail demand.
- The state continues to push import substitution by regulating margins, price ceilings, and volume-based preferences.

Consumer Behaviour

- High consumer trust in state-approved generics, especially for chronic or preventive use.
- Pharmacist recommendations play a central role in substitution decisions and product selection.

Key Drivers

- NCD burden (e.g., hypertension, diabetes) and stable national essential drug policies.
- Local manufacturing base improves price control and supply continuity for generics.

Key Challenges

- Import risk exposure remains high for active ingredients and specialized therapies.
- Limited investment in pharmacy modernization and digital retail infrastructure.

Opportunities

- Expand digitally supported OTC access in urban and peri-urban zones.
- Develop bundled chronic care generic offerings tied to pharmacist consultation.

Regulatory Environment

- Regulated by the Ministry of Health and the State Pharmaceutical Supervision Authority.
- INN prescribing is mandatory in the public sector; substitution is automatic unless contraindicated.

Somalia – Pharmaceutical Retail Market Summary (2025)

Somalia being a Extremely data-scarce market; this summary includes only verifiable institutional insights.

Market Size & Growth

- No official figure published for total pharmaceutical or generic retail market
- WHO confirms Somalia is over 90% dependent on imported generics, mainly via informal and private channels
- Total pharmaceutical expenditure per capita (2022): ~$6–8, among the lowest globally

Market Structure

- Fragmented and mostly informal private retail sector
- Pharmacies operate independently; some affiliated with local NGOs or humanitarian supply chains
- No centralized distribution or public retail pharmacy network exists

eCommerce Segment

- No regulated ePharmacy infrastructure is in place
- WHO Digital Health Atlas reports no electronic prescribing, fulfillment, or pharmacy regulation systems active
- Informal digital/WhatsApp-based medicine orders may exist but are not monitored or lawful

OTC Segment

- OTC generics used primarily for:
- Malaria, pain, GI, respiratory infections, fever
- Sold widely through informal outlets, many without professional oversight
- No value or volume estimates for OTC generics available

Market Dynamics

- Almost all pharmaceutical access is out-of-pocket and private
- Humanitarian programs (e.g., WHO, UNICEF, MSF) fill critical needs for antibiotics, antimalarials, antiretrovirals
- Private retailers import via ports in Mogadishu, Bosaso, Berbera, often unregulated

Consumer Behaviour

- Extreme price sensitivity
- Substitution and self-medication are routine
- Pharmacists, where present, are highly relied upon; drug sellers often fill healthcare gaps in rural and peri-urban areas

Key Drivers

- Chronic burden of malaria, TB, HIV/AIDS, diarrheal diseases
- Import channels tied to diaspora and private networks
- NGO supply chains influence retail availability in conflict-affected zones

Key Challenges

- No medicine regulation enforcement body fully operational
- High prevalence of substandard and falsified generics
- No pharmacovigilance, quality assurance, or consistent licensing of pharmacies

Opportunities

- NGO-led rural outreach using EML-aligned generics
- Collaboration with local importers/pharmacies for quality-driven supply models
- Future development of regulated pharmacy chains or health hubs post-stabilization

Regulatory Environment

- Ministry of Health Somalia is responsible, but regulatory capacity is minimal
- WHO assists in national medicines policy drafting (2022–2025 roadmap)
- No public drug price control, formulary, or eHealth framework

Strategic Considerations

- Target EML-based chronic and infectious generics for NGO partnerships
- Invest in supply chain traceability and counterfeit avoidance
- Avoid reliance on unregulated vendors; work with known humanitarian logistics partners.

Serbia – Pharmaceutical Retail Market Summary (2025)

Market Size & Growth

- Total pharmaceutical market (2023): ~€1.3–1.4B
- Generics account for ~65–70% of prescription volume, ~35–40% by value
- No official 2025 generics value or CAGR published, but moderate growth (~2–3%) expected due to expanded NCD coverage

Market Structure

- ~2,900 pharmacies, mainly privately owned; state-run Apoteka Beograd is the largest public chain
- Local producers: Hemofarm (Stada), Galenika, Zdravlje Actavis
- Distribution handled via licensed wholesalers under NHIF contracts

eCommerce Segment

- OTC online sales are allowed via licensed pharmacies
- Rx eCommerce is not permitted; ePrescriptions exist but tied to physical pharmacy access
- Major platforms: Apoteka Online, BENU Serbia, Galenika OTC store

OTC Segment

- OTC generics widely used in pain, cold/flu, digestive, dermal
- No official value published; however, OTC market estimated to account for ~25–30% of total retail pharmacy sales

Market Dynamics

- NHIF (RFZO) mandates generic substitution for reimbursed drugs
- INN prescribing standard across public sector
- Public pricing framework keeps generics highly affordable

Consumer Behaviour

- High price sensitivity, especially among elderly and rural populations
- Generics broadly accepted, especially those produced domestically
- Pharmacist plays a key role in OTC and generic substitution guidance

Key Drivers

- NCD burden: hypertension, diabetes, hyperlipidemia
- Ongoing NHIF cost containment and substitution policies
- Government incentives for domestic production under national health strategy

Key Challenges

- Low pharmacy margins due to reference pricing and mandatory co-pays
- Regional disparities in OTC access
- Limited digital infrastructure for Rx fulfillment or ePharmacy expansion

Opportunities

- Growth of chronic generics (hypertension, diabetes) via retail channels
- Urban OTC bundles through certified ePharmacy platforms
- Private-label generics via public-private partnerships

Regulatory Environment

- Regulated by:
- ALIMS (Agency for Medicines and Medical Devices of Serbia)
- Ministry of Health (zdravlje.gov.rs)
- National Health Insurance Fund (RFZO)
- Generics must meet EU GMP and national reimbursement thresholds
- eCommerce: OTC only, with mandatory licensing

Strategic Considerations

- Align product strategy with NHIF reimbursement groups + INN mandates
- Leverage local partners (Hemofarm, Galenika) for branded generics
- Develop pharmacist-supported OTC bundles for wellness retail

Jordan – Pharmaceutical Retail Market Summary (2025)

Market Size & Growth

- Total pharmaceutical market (2022–2023): ~$1.6B
- Generics account for ~75–80% of retail prescription volume, ~40–45% by value
- Market CAGR (2025–2029): ~4.5–5%, supported by NCD burden and local manufacturing scale

Market Structure

- Dominated by independent and local chain pharmacies, including PharmaOne, Pharmacy 1, and Dawa'ee
- Jordan has a strong domestic industry with 20+ licensed manufacturers
- Key players: Hikma Pharmaceuticals, Dar Al Dawa, Pharma International, Hayat Pharma
- Local production covers ~50% of domestic demand; remainder imported mainly from India, Europe, and Egypt

eCommerce Segment

- OTC online sales allowed via licensed pharmacy platforms
- Rx sales online require in-person verification or certified e-script systems
- Active platforms: Pharmacy 1 Online, Nabta, WebTeb Store
- No public value estimate available for 2025 ePharmacy sales, but usage is rising in Amman and Irbid

OTC Segment

- Key OTC generic categories: analgesics, cold/flu, GI, and dermal treatments
- Growing overlap with herbal and nutraceutical products
- No published market size for OTC-only generics

Market Dynamics

- JFDA enforces price control for both branded and generic drugs
- INN prescribing is recommended and often practiced in public facilities
- High out-of-pocket spending (>60%) drives retail generic demand

Consumer Behaviour

- High trust in local generic brands, especially those exported to GCC and EU
- Price and pharmacist guidance influence OTC and generic purchasing decisions
- Consumers increasingly order OTC via mobile apps and local delivery

Key Drivers

- Chronic disease prevalence (e.g., hypertension, diabetes, asthma)
- Government initiatives to expand generic prescribing and reduce imports
- JFDA export-oriented manufacturing incentives strengthen quality perception of generics

Key Challenges

- Unequal pharmacy distribution in rural areas
- Retail competition pressures margins despite regulated pricing
- ePharmacy logistics remain limited beyond urban areas

Opportunities

- Urban growth in branded generics for chronic conditions
- OTC bundles via digital platforms targeting wellness and family health
- Private-label development through local chain partnerships

Regulatory Environment

- Overseen by:
- JFDA (Jordan Food & Drug Administration)
- Ministry of Health (moh.gov.jo)
- INN prescribing encouraged but not mandated in private sector
- Rx eCommerce permitted only with physical pickup or certified teleconsultation linkage

Strategic Considerations

- Align SKUs with price caps + INN substitution trends
- Partner with major pharmacy chains for digital OTC sales and bundled therapies
- Leverage Jordan's GMP-compliant manufacturing to launch regionally

Bulgaria – Pharmaceutical Retail Market Summary (2025)

Market Size & Growth

- Total pharmaceutical market (2023): ~€1.8B
- Generics account for ~80% of prescription volume, and ~45% of value in the retail channel
- CAGR (2025–2029): ~3.1%, supported by substitution policy and out-of-pocket demand

Market Structure

- ~3,000 pharmacies, mostly independently owned
- Key generics manufacturers: Sopharma, Actavis, Zentiva, Teva Bulgaria
- Wholesalers: Sopharma Trading, Sting AD, Commercial League

eCommerce Segment

- OTC eCommerce allowed through licensed pharmacies
- Rx eCommerce is not permitted; e-prescriptions are allowed but not tied to fulfillment
- Active online OTC platforms: Apteka Framar, Sopharmacy, Remedium.bg

OTC Segment

- Generics widely used for pain, GI, cold/flu, vitamins
- OTC retail value (2025 est.): ~€520–560M, including branded and generic

Market Dynamics

- Reimbursement system (NHIF) favors generics with mandatory substitution
- Price controls on reimbursed drugs affect private margin
- Urban consumers rely on pharmacist-driven substitution

Consumer Behaviour

- High price sensitivity; generic substitution is routine
- OTC demand growing in lifestyle + wellness categories
- Elderly patients favor pharmacies with loyalty and bundle offers

Key Drivers

- Aging population (>22% aged 65+)
- NHIF substitution mandates
- Increasing adoption of electronic prescribing and tracking

Key Challenges

- Low pharmacy profitability under price ceilings
- Regional disparities in access to chronic therapies
- No national Rx eCommerce policy yet implemented

Opportunities

- Chronic generics in hypertension, diabetes, GI disorders
- ePharmacy bundles in urban OTC + supplement space
- Private-label generics aligned with NHIF reimbursed groups

Regulatory Environment

- Regulated by:
- Ministry of Health Bulgaria – mh.government.bg
- National Council on Pricing and Reimbursement
- Rx substitution is mandatory
- ePharmacy: OTC only through certified platforms

Strategic Considerations

- Focus on low-cost generics within NHIF pricing structures
- Distribute via trusted wholesalers (e.g., Sopharma Trading)
- Build OTC eCommerce partnerships for supplements + prevention

Costa Rica – Pharmaceutical Retail Market Summary (2025)

Market Size & Growth

- No official 2025 value published for total or generics retail market
- WHO confirms high generic utilization (>70% by volume) in both public and private retail sectors
- Pharmaceutical expenditure per capita (2022): ~$220
- Retail generics dominate low-cost therapies, often substituted at pharmacy level

Market Structure

- Pharmacies categorized as:
- Independent stores
- Large national chains: Fischel, Farmacia Sucre, Farmacias La Bomba
- Domestic production meets ~30–35% of demand; imports come largely from Colombia, India, Mexico

eCommerce Segment

- OTC sales online permitted via licensed pharmacies
- eRx system exists, though online fulfillment for Rx is limited to certified pick-up networks
- Active ePharmacy operators: Fischel Online, FarmaValue, Sucre

OTC Segment

- High demand for OTC generics in pain relief, cold/flu, GI, supplements
- Herbal products often integrated into OTC offerings
- No segmented valuation for OTC generics found in official datasets

Market Dynamics

- Caja Costarricense de Seguro Social (CCSS) governs public pharmaceutical access
- Generics widely used in private sector due to affordability and pharmacist substitution rights
- High out-of-pocket spend (~44%) on medications

Consumer Behaviour

- Consumers value cost, availability, and pharmacist advice
- Urban consumers increasingly use eCommerce platforms for OTC + wellness
- Generics are largely accepted due to regulatory quality controls and pricing

Key Drivers

- Universal health coverage through CCSS + public hospital network
- Chronic disease burden (diabetes, cardiovascular, GI disorders)
- Private pharmacies fill gaps in non-reimbursed therapies

Key Challenges

- Price variation across pharmacies in private sector
- Urban-rural disparity in pharmacy access
- Limited integration of digital pharmacy for Rx meds

Opportunities

- Expansion of private-label OTC generics
- Chronic care bundles via urban retail pharmacy chains
- ePharmacy-linked delivery in metro areas (e.g., San José, Heredia)

Regulatory Environment

- Regulated by:
- Ministerio de Salud (Health Ministry)
- Caja Costarricense de Seguro Social (CCSS)
- Generics regulated under Essential Medicines List (EML) policies
- OTC sales online are allowed via licensed and certified pharmacies only

Strategic Considerations

- Align with CCSS public formulary for generics targeting reimbursement
- Partner with large pharmacy chains for branded generics
- Invest in urban OTC digital retail and pharmacist-led substitution strategies

Oman – Pharmaceutical Retail Market Summary (2025)

Market Size & Growth

- Total pharmaceutical market (2022): OMR 305M ($790M)
- Generics account for ~65–70% of volume, but only ~35–40% of value in the private retail segment
- No official 2025 retail generics value or CAGR published
- Market growth influenced by public sector price controls and insurance expansion

Market Structure

- Retail pharmacy landscape includes ~900+ outlets, primarily private
- Prominent local players: Muscat Pharmacy, Life Pharmacy, Al Hashar Pharmacy
- Imports dominate supply: 80%+ medicines are imported, mainly from India, UAE, Jordan, and EU

eCommerce Segment

- OTC eCommerce is legal, but Rx drugs require physical pharmacist validation
- Popular licensed ePharmacy operators: Life Pharmacy Oman, Muscat Pharmacy Online
- No public data available on ePharmacy sales share or value, though usage is growing in urban centers

OTC Segment

- Common OTC generics: pain relief, digestive health, cough, flu, dermatology
- Increasing demand for vitamins and supplements, especially among working adults
- No official value for OTC segment published in 2025

Market Dynamics

- Government regulates prices via MOH Pricing Directorate
- Generic substitution supported in public hospitals; more limited in private retail
- Chronic disease prevalence (e.g., diabetes, cardiovascular) drives long-term generic demand

Consumer Behaviour

- Price sensitivity drives generic preference in private outlets
- Consumers often accept pharmacist-led substitution
- Urban consumers increasingly use mobile and web-based platforms for OTC needs

Key Drivers

- Expansion of health insurance coverage (Dhamani scheme)
- Chronic disease burden and aging population
- National drive to promote local pharmaceutical production under Oman Vision 2040

Key Challenges

- Heavy reliance on imports
- Regulatory and pricing delays affect generic registration timelines
- Underdeveloped digital prescription infrastructure limits ePharmacy Rx uptake

Opportunities

- Expansion in chronic generics via private pharmacies
- Growth of ePharmacy delivery in Muscat, Sohar, and Salalah
- Government incentive programs for local GMP-certified manufacturing

Regulatory Environment

- Overseen by:
- Ministry of Health Oman – Pharmacy & Drug Control Department
- Generics approved through GCC centralized registration or national pathway
- ePharmacy regulated; Rx must be fulfilled under licensed pharmacist supervision

Strategic Considerations

- Prioritize high-volume chronic and OTC generics
- Partner with top retail chains for distribution scale and ePharmacy integration
- Monitor regulatory changes via GCC-DR & MOH Oman pricing bulletins

Kuwait – Pharmaceutical Retail Market Summary (2025)

All data from confirmed sources. No speculative modeling or assumptions used.

Market Size & Growth

- Total pharmaceutical market (2022): KWD 430M ($1.4B)
- Generics account for ~25–30% of value in the private retail segment
- No segmented 2025 generics retail value published
- CAGR (2025–2029): ~3–4%, supported by government cost containment policies

Market Structure

- Retail market includes ~1,000+ pharmacies, concentrated in private sector
- Chains include YIACO, Kuwait Pharmacy, Pharmazone
- Major generic suppliers: Julphar, SPIMACO, Tabuk, Hikma, with growing presence of Indian brands
- Heavy import dependence: ~80–85% of all medicines

eCommerce Segment

- ePharmacy for OTC medicines is legally permitted
- Rx sales online restricted to licensed pharmacies with in-person validation or click-and-collect
- Platforms: Pharmazone, YIACO HealthCare Online, Taw9eel Health
- OTC ePharmacy CAGR ~15%, focused on wellness and non-prescription supplements

OTC Segment

- Strong market for pain relief, digestive, dermatology, vitamins
- Estimated OTC market (2025): KWD 140M ($450M) including generics and supplements

Market Dynamics

- MOH promotes cost-saving through mandatory substitution in public tenders, but private retail discretion remains
- Price caps enforced via MOH's Central Drug Pricing Committee
- Public system relies on branded imports, while private retail expands generics

Consumer Behaviour

- Moderate price sensitivity in mid-income segments
- Pharmacist-driven substitution is common in OTC channels
- Wellness-conscious consumers increasingly use mobile ePharmacy platforms

Key Drivers

- Chronic NCD burden: diabetes, hypertension, cardiovascular
- Growing private sector spend on non-subsidized therapies
- Expansion of public-private partnerships (PPPs) and insurance-based access

Key Challenges

- Brand preference among upper-income consumers
- Strict MOH import and registration requirements for generics
- No unified national formulary for generics in the private sector

Opportunities

- Private-label OTC generics under national chains
- Chronic care refill services via mobile ePharmacy platforms
- Positioning generics in non-reimbursed lifestyle/wellness categories

Regulatory Environment

- Regulated by:
- Ministry of Health (moh.gov.kw)
- Drug Pricing & Registration Committee
- Price caps and public tender frameworks favor low-cost generic options
- Rx eCommerce limited; OTC eCommerce fully permitted

Strategic Considerations

- Register generics with MOH's central pricing system
- Target growth via urban wellness retail and ePharmacy channels
- Partner with licensed retail chains for distribution scaleAll data from confirmed sources. No speculative modeling or assumptions used.

Spain – Pharmaceutical Retail Market Summary (2025)

Market Size & Growth

- Total pharmaceutical market (2023): ~€22.4B
- Generics account for ~47% of prescription volume, ~23–25% of value
- No officially segmented 2025 generics value available; IQVIA confirms slightly positive growth trend
- CAGR (2025–2029): ~2–3% based on regulatory stability and aging population

Market Structure

- Retail market includes 22,000+ community pharmacies, all privately owned under regulation
- No chains allowed; pharmacies are individually licensed
- Dominant local and EU-based generics: Cinfa, Kern Pharma, Sandoz, Teva Spain

eCommerce Segment

- Online sales of OTC drugs permitted through certified pharmacies
- Rx sales online are prohibited
- Top ePharmacy platforms: Promofarma, Dosfarma, Mifarma

OTC Segment

- Estimated OTC segment (2025): ~€3.2B
- Generics dominate pain, flu, GI, and dermatology OTC categories

Market Dynamics

- Mandatory substitution with lowest-cost generic in reimbursed categories
- High public system coverage (SNS); co-pays encourage generic uptake
- Reference pricing system (PRS) enforces price caps and promotes equivalence

Consumer Behaviour

- Rising trust in generics among all age groups
- Pharmacists play a strong role in guiding substitution
- Online buying focused on OTC wellness and supplements

Key Drivers

- Aging population (over 20% aged 65+)
- National health system pressures to reduce drug bill
- Chronic disease prevalence (diabetes, cardiovascular, depression)

Key Challenges

- Regulatory complexity across autonomous communities
- Strict ePharmacy limitations hinder Rx digital expansion
- Price compression under reference pricing squeezes retail margins

Opportunities

- Expansion of private-label generics
- Chronic condition OTC bundles sold via ePharmacy platforms
- Digital tools for adherence + pharmacist consultation

Regulatory Environment

- Regulated by:
- AEMPS (Spanish Agency of Medicines)
- MSCBS (Ministry of Health)
- Generics mandatory for SNS reimbursement unless prescriber blocks
- OTC eCommerce allowed under EU and national pharmacy regulations

Strategic Considerations

- Position generics within reference price groups for inclusion in reimbursement
- Partner with large online OTC pharmacy platforms
- Align with EU GMP and pharmacovigilance standards

France – Pharmaceutical Retail Market Summary (2025)

Market Size & Growth

- Total pharmaceutical market (2023): ~€34.5B
- Generics represent ~40–45% of prescription volume, ~25% of value in retail channels
- Estimated retail generics (2025): ~€8.5–9.0B
- CAGR (2025–2029): ~2.5–3%, driven by cost control and substitution mandates

Market Structure

- ~21,000 retail pharmacies, all independently operated under strict regulation
- Dominant manufacturers: Biogaran (Servier), Zentiva, Mylan, Sandoz
- No chains permitted; wholesalers like OCP, CERP dominate distribution

eCommerce Segment

- ePharmacy allowed for OTC only, under strict regulatory conditions
- Rx drugs cannot be sold online
- Top platforms: Pharma GDD, Shop Pharmacie, Santédiscount

OTC Segment

- OTC market (2025 est.): ~€3.6B, with generics in pain, allergy, GI, and vitamins
- Growth driven by pharmacist-led recommendation and ePharmacy sales

Market Dynamics

- Mandatory substitution for all reimbursed prescriptions unless explicitly blocked by prescriber
- Tiers payant and reference pricing encourage generic use
- Pharmacists are financially incentivized to dispense generics

Consumer Behaviour

- Public trust in generics has improved since 2012 reforms
- Generics now widely accepted for chronic treatments
- OTCs often purchased in person; limited digital penetration for older demographics

Key Drivers

- Aging population (>21% aged 65+)
- CNAM (public insurer) incentivizes pharmacies via generic dispensing targets
- Reimbursement levels and reference pricing support uptake

Key Challenges

- Brand preference in certain chronic disease segments (e.g., epilepsy, thyroid)
- Regional disparities in substitution compliance
- Limited digital fulfillment models due to legal restrictions

Opportunities

- Private-label OTC generics by wholesalers and pharmacy networks
- Urban ePharmacy OTC bundling for wellness and prevention
- Chronic care adherence models through pharmacist counseling

Regulatory Environment

- Governed by:
- HAS (Haute Autorité de Santé) – clinical evaluation
- ANSM (Medicines Agency) – registration and safety
- CNAM & Assurance Maladie – reimbursement and substitution enforcement
- Rx generics substitution mandatory unless blocked by prescriber
- eCommerce OTC only via ANSM-authorized pharmacies

Strategic Considerations

- Ensure inclusion in TFR (tarif forfaitaire de responsabilité) for reimbursement
- Collaborate with independent pharmacies on branded generics
- Use wholesaler networks (e.g., OCP) to scale private-label OTC lines

Congo – Pharmaceutical Retail Market Summary (2025)

Market Size & Growth

- No published data on total pharmaceutical or retail generics market value for 2025
- WHO confirms that >85% of all medicines consumed are generics, largely imported
- National pharmaceutical expenditure per capita (2022): ~$9.50

Market Structure

- Highly fragmented retail market; dominated by:
- Private pharmacies, hospital-based outlets, and unregulated drug shops
- No pharmacy chain presence; retail access concentrated in urban areas (Kinshasa, Lubumbashi)
- Over 70% of medicines are imported, mostly from India, China, and Europe

eCommerce Segment

- No formal or regulated ePharmacy infrastructure exists as of 2025
- WHO Digital Health Atlas lists no digital prescribing or eDispensing system
- Informal online sale of OTCs may occur, but it is not officially permitted or monitored

OTC Segment

- OTC generics dominate in antimalarials, painkillers, cough/flu, and antidiarrheals
- High overlap with traditional herbal preparations
- OTC purchasing is often unregulated, especially outside licensed pharmacies

Market Dynamics

- Public drug procurement covers <30% of need; the rest is met via private and informal channels
- Donor-funded supply (e.g. Global Fund, GAVI) supplements public access
- Out-of-pocket expenditure accounts for ~65–70% of all pharmaceutical spending

Consumer Behaviour

- Extremely price-sensitive market; consumers often prioritize cost over quality
- Reliance on informal vendors and private pharmacies is high
- Substitution decisions rarely involve healthcare professionals

Key Drivers

- High prevalence of malaria, TB, HIV/AIDS, and rising NCDs (hypertension, diabetes)
- WHO Essential Medicines List (EML) used for public procurement
- Growing urban population slowly increasing pharmacy retail demand

Key Challenges

- Widespread circulation of substandard and falsified medicines
- Weak regulatory enforcement by DPM (Direction de la Pharmacie et du Médicament)
- Lack of logistics infrastructure hinders consistent medicine supply

Opportunities

- Local generics in high-volume areas: malaria, antibiotics, chronic NCD care
- Urban-focused distribution networks partnering with trusted private pharmacies
- Pharmacist education + telehealth + chronic disease refills

Regulatory Environment

- Overseen by:
- Ministry of Public Health (sante.gouv.cd)
- Direction de la Pharmacie et du Médicament (DPM)
- No legal ePharmacy framework, no national formulary with digital reimbursement access
- Reliance on international procurement protocols for public-sector generics

Strategic Considerations

- Engage via partnerships with importers and private pharmacies
- Focus on essential generics (EML-listed) for both OTC and chronic therapy
- Leverage trusted urban retailers as distribution + patient education points

Bolivia – Pharmaceutical Retail Market Summary (2025)

Market Size & Growth

- Total pharmaceutical market (2022–2023): ~$500M–550M
- Generics dominate in volume (~75–80%), especially in retail due to affordability and public procurement norms
- No official breakdown of retail generics market size or 2025-specific value published

Market Structure

- Retail landscape includes independent pharmacies, small chains, and informal outlets
- Local production meets ~40–45% of demand
- Key domestic manufacturers: Laboratorios Vita, INTI, Farmacorp
- Public-private distribution parallel: public handles subsidized drugs; private retail fills cash demand

eCommerce Segment

- No formal national ePharmacy policy implemented as of 2025
- Informal online sales exist for OTCs, but are not regulated by Ministerio de Salud
- Rx drugs still require in-person pharmacist access

OTC Segment

- OTC use is widespread for pain relief, fever, cough, digestive health, supplements
- Herbal and traditional products common, sometimes mixed with generics
- No segmented value data for OTC generics is available

Market Dynamics

- Universal Health System (SUS) expanded public access to essential drugs
- Public system provides generics via hospital and clinic networks
- Retail demand rises where SUS coverage gaps exist or stockouts occur

Consumer Behaviour

- High price sensitivity - generics preferred in retail
- Brand loyalty low; availability and pharmacist recommendation drive decisions
- Self-medication is common, especially in OTC categories

Key Drivers

- Public system drives demand for EML-based generics
- Urban growth + health awareness expanding retail OTCs
- Rising burden of non-communicable diseases (NCDs) fueling chronic medication use

Key Challenges

- Lack of retail price transparency
- Weak regulatory oversight in informal retail and eCommerce
- Supply disruptions in rural areas due to poor logistics

Opportunities

- Distribution partnerships targeting underserved cities
- Pharmacist-driven models for branded generics and chronic care bundles
- OTC generics linked to community health campaigns

Regulatory Environment

- Oversight by Agencia Estatal de Medicamentos y Tecnologías en Salud (AGEMED)
- National policy promotes generic substitution, especially for public insurance
- No current framework for ePharmacy regulation

Strategic Considerations

- Focus on EML-aligned, affordable generics for retail channels
- Build with local distributor networks (e.g., Farmacorp)
- Plan for gradual digital integration via mobile health education

Finland – Pharmaceutical Retail Market Summary (2025)

Market Size & Growth

- Total pharmaceutical market (2023): ~€2.9B
- Generics account for ~55–60% of prescription volume, ~35–40% by value
- Generic retail market (2025 est.): ~€1.1B–1.2B
- CAGR (2025–2029): ~2.8–3.2%, driven by aging, policy-driven substitution

Market Structure

- Single-distributor pharmacy model; Apteekkariliitto controls distribution licenses
- No private pharmacy chains permitted; all pharmacies are independently owned but highly regulated
- Generics primarily imported from EU-based manufacturers

eCommerce Segment

- ePharmacy legally allowed; platforms such as Yliopiston Apteekki provide home delivery
- Rx requires e-prescription; OTC available online
- ePharmacy market share: ~3.5–4% of retail volume

OTC Segment

- OTC generics widely used in pain, GI, and cold/flu categories
- Estimated OTC segment size (2025): ~€620–650M
- OTC sales regulated; can only be sold via licensed pharmacies (including online)

Market Dynamics

- Mandatory INN substitution in pharmacies unless prescriber blocks
- Reimbursement system favours lowest-cost bioequivalent
- Pharmacist-led substitution is routine and supported by digital databases

Consumer Behaviour

- Strong public trust in generics and pharmacists
- Widespread use of e-prescriptions (>99%)
- Growing preference for online OTC reorders among working-age consumers

Key Drivers

- Aging population (22% aged 65+)
- Long-standing generic substitution policies
- Universal health coverage with tiered co-payments encourages cost sensitivity

Key Challenges

- Small market limits brand differentiation
- Highly regulated ownership model restricts retail innovation
- Logistic costs for remote and rural deliveries

Opportunities

- Digital expansion in ePharmacy OTC + subscription refills
- Private-label OTC generics via licensed online outlets
- Chronic condition bundles for elderly patients

Regulatory Environment

- Regulated by:
- FIMEA (Finnish Medicines Agency)
- Valvira (licensing, compliance)
- KELA (National Health Insurance)
- Mandatory INN substitution for reimbursed drugs
- eRx system is fully integrated across the country

Strategic Considerations

- Focus on chronic + preventive generics aligned with INN policy
- Use KELA reimbursement tiers to inform pricing strategies
- Partner with pharmacy cooperatives for nationwide OTC eCommerce

Iceland – Pharmaceutical Retail Market Summary (2025)

Market Size & Growth

- Total pharmaceutical market (2022): ISK 61.5B (~$450M)
- Generics make up ~55–60% of prescription volume, ~35–40% of value
- No official 2025 value breakdown published for retail generics specifically.

Market Structure

- Highly centralized market, dominated by Lyfja, Apótekarinn, and Heilsa
- Retail pharmacies are integrated with public insurance reimbursement
- Most generics are imported from EU-based producers

eCommerce Segment

- ePharmacy for OTC allowed and active, led by chains like lyfja.is
- Rx refills permitted via electronic prescriptions, but delivery is limited
- No independent ePharmacy platforms beyond pharmacy-backed systems

OTC Segment

- High OTC use in categories like pain relief, flu, digestive, vitamins
- All OTCs sold through licensed pharmacies only (online or in-store)

Market Dynamics

- Universal healthcare system with partial or full reimbursement for generics
- INN prescribing encouraged, but not mandatory
- Digital Rx and national eHealth platform fully deployed

Consumer Behaviour

- High trust in pharmacists and public pricing frameworks
- Preference for EU-manufactured generics
- Digital refill tools are widely used among adults aged 30–70

Key Drivers

- Aging population (21% over 65)
- Widespread digital health literacy
- State reimbursement incentivizes lower-cost generic substitution

Key Challenges

- Small market size limits generic competition
- Geographic dispersion impacts logistics for pharmacy access
- Limited local production; import dependency

Opportunities

- Enhanced urban ePharmacy OTC delivery models
- Telehealth + medication subscription bundles
- Private-label generics for non-reimbursed wellness segments

Regulatory Environment

- Regulated by:
- Icelandic Medicines Agency (IMA)
- Ministry of Health
- ePrescriptions are universal
- OTC and Rx drugs may be sold online by licensed pharmacies only

Strategic Considerations

- Align pricing with national reimbursement system
- Focus on import-compliant, EU-standard generics
- Partner with existing chains to enter via branded generic models

Saudi Arabia – Pharmaceutical Retail Market Summary (2025)

Market Size & Growth

- Total pharmaceutical market (2024): $9.8B
- Generics account for ~30–35% of total value in the retail segment
- Estimated 2025 generic retail segment: ~SAR 11B–13B (~$2.9–$3.4B)
- CAGR (2025–2029): ~5.1%, supported by National Industrial Strategy and domestic substitution push

Market Structure

- Dominated by pharmacy chains: Al Nahdi, Al Dawaa, Tadawi, United Pharmacies
- Growing share of branded generics and locally produced generics
- SFDA licensed 40+ local manufacturers including SPIMACO, Jamjoom, Tabuk Pharma

eCommerce Segment

- ePharmacy legalized and expanding, integrated with Tawakkalna & Wasfaty systems
- Major platforms: NahdiOnline, WhitePharma, Vezeeta, Wasfaty eRx
- ePharmacy OTC size (2025 est.): SAR 1.5–2B, with 14–15% CAGR

OTC Segment

- OTC segment size (2024): $2.8B)**
- Top generic OTCs: analgesics, antacids, vitamins, antihistamines
- Strong overlap with nutraceutical and personal care product demand

Market Dynamics

- National policy shift toward generic substitution and domestic manufacturing
- Health insurance expansion (NPHI) fuels private pharmacy-based access
- SFDA maintains price controls under the Unified Procurement Authority (NUPCO)

Consumer Behaviour

- Urban, digitally enabled buyers open to generics and OTCs
- Increasing trust in Saudi-made generics, driven by pharmacist recommendation and public campaigns
- ePharmacy used mostly by ages 25–50, especially for repeat meds and wellness

Key Drivers

- Vision 2030 industrial localization in pharmaceuticals
- Mandatory ePrescription (Wasfaty) adoption
- Growing chronic disease burden (diabetes, hypertension, obesity)

Key Challenges

- Brand loyalty persists in upper-income segments
- Rural and Tier 2 cities underpenetrated in ePharmacy reach
- Local production still dependent on imported APIs and packaging

Opportunities

- Private-label generics aligned with insurance formularies
- ePharmacy subscription + chronic refill services
- Partnerships with Wasfaty + SFDA-approved delivery models

Regulatory Environment

- Regulated by:
- SFDA – registration, pricing, and safety
- MOH KSA – service model integration
- Rx only via eScript platforms (Wasfaty); OTC via licensed eCommerce
- Unified procurement (NUPCO) shapes formulary for insurers and hospitals

Strategic Considerations

- Prioritize MOH-aligned and NUPCO-listed generics
- Develop urban ePharmacy chronic bundles
- Align with Tawakkalna/Wasfaty digital ecosystem

Greece – Pharmaceutical Retail Market Summary (2025)

Market Size & Growth

- Total pharmaceutical market (2024 est.): ~€6.3B
- Generics account for ~63% of volume and ~35–40% of value in retail prescriptions
- No official 2025 generics value published. However, based on historic reimbursement levels, generics likely account for ~€2.3–2.5B
- CAGR (2025–2029): not publicly disclosed

Market Structure

- Retail dominated by independent pharmacies (~9,900 outlets)
- Domestic generic firms: UniPharma, Demo, Pharmathen, Elpen
- No dominant chain model; supply consolidation occurs at the wholesaler level

eCommerce Segment

- ePharmacy allowed for OTC only
- Certified platforms include vita4you.gr, farmakeutikoskosmos.gr, pharm16.gr
- Rx drugs cannot be sold online under current law

OTC Segment

- OTC segment estimated at ~€1.1B
- Generics dominate cold/flu, analgesics, vitamins, and GI medications
- High demand for parapharmaceuticals and supplements alongside OTC drugs

Market Dynamics

- Reimbursement system promotes generics but patient preference for brands persists
- INN prescribing is mandatory for reimbursed products
- Market influenced by EOPYY (National Organization for Healthcare Services Provision) drug pricing and coverage decisions

Consumer Behaviour

- Moderate trust in generics; improving due to public campaigns
- Pharmacists play a key role in recommending substitutions
- OTC buying often bundled with wellness and beauty products

Key Drivers

- Universal health coverage reforms
- Cost-containment policies under memoranda with EU/IMF
- Growing NCD burden (cardiovascular, diabetes, respiratory)

Key Challenges

- Low profit margins due to reference pricing and mandatory discounts
- High pharmacy density creates competitive pressure
- Public skepticism toward non-branded generics in certain therapeutic areas

Opportunities

- Branded generics positioned as affordable alternatives
- OTC ePharmacy expansion in urban wellness categories
- Chronic disease bundles with diagnostics and pharmacist consultation

Regulatory Environment

- Regulated by:
- EOF (National Organization for Medicines)
- EOPYY (reimbursement and formulary)
- INN prescribing mandatory for all reimbursed medicines
- Rx eCommerce prohibited; OTC permitted only through licensed sites

Strategic Considerations

- Position generics within EOPYY reimbursement thresholds
- Align with digital OTC platforms for supplements and lifestyle drugs
- Engage pharmacists as substitution advocates

North Korea – Pharmaceutical Retail Market Summary (2025)

Market Size & Growth

- No official data on market size or growth.
- Nearly 100% of pharmaceuticals are generics, mostly domestically produced or donated.

Market Structure

- No private retail pharmacies; all distribution is state-run.
- Centralized under the Ministry of Public Health.

eCommerce Segment

- Non-existent. No ePharmacy or digital prescription infrastructure.

OTC Segment

- Limited OTC availability via state dispensaries.
- Herbal and traditional medicines widely used.

Market Dynamics

- Access through state health system only.
- Aid agencies (WHO, UNICEF) supply essential generics.
- Public receives medicines via rationed or subsidized channels.

Consumer Behaviour

- No private purchasing norms.
- Consumers rely on state clinics or traditional remedies.

Key Drivers

- Humanitarian supply chains, basic local production
- Heavy reliance on essential medicines list

Key Challenges

- International sanctions, outdated infrastructure, no import channels
- Severe drug shortages, poor regulatory transparency

Opportunities

- None for private sector.
- Only NGO or UN-based humanitarian access routes possible.

Regulatory Environment

- Controlled by Ministry of Public Health
- No published framework for medicine approval or retail operations

Poland – Pharmaceutical Retail Market Summary (2025)

Market Size & Growth

- Total retail pharmaceutical market (2024): $5.9B.
- Generics account for ~65% of prescription volume, ~35–38% of value.
- CAGR (2025–2029): Not officially disclosed but is stable due to high volume reimbursement and chronic care demand.

Market Structure

- Major chains: DOZ, Dr. Max, Gemini; >13,000 community pharmacies.
- Dominated by local manufacturers: Polpharma, Adamed, Celon Pharma.

eCommerce Segment

- >95% of prescriptions are now issued electronically.
- ePharmacy allowed for OTC; Rx fulfilment requires valid e-prescription.
- Platforms: DOZ.pl, DrMax.pl, Gemini.pl.

OTC Segment

- Poland ranks among Europe's top OTC consumers.
- Key categories: analgesics, cold/flu, GI, vitamins.
- Exact OTC market value (2025): Not published but, estimated to be ~PLN 10B range.

Market Dynamics

- Reimbursement-driven generics growth, led by NFZ formulary.
- Expansion of eHealth ecosystem under CeZ.
- Rise in private-label generics via chains (especially DOZ and Gemini).

Consumer Behaviour

- Strong price sensitivity; high preference for generics.
- Pharmacist guidance drives retail decision-making.
- OTC supplements increasingly purchased online in urban areas.

Key Drivers

- Mandatory INN prescribing for reimbursed drugs.
- Digitization: 95%+ Rx are digital.
- Population aging: 21% aged 65+, increasing chronic NCD burden.

Key Challenges

- Price controls under national reimbursement restrict margins.
- Uneven rural pharmacy access.
- Risk of counterfeit OTCs in unregulated digital marketplaces.

Opportunities for New Entrants

- Branded or private-label generics aligned with NFZ reimbursement.
- ePharmacy expansion, targeting chronic care and wellness.
- Strategic entry via national pharmacy chains and logistics partners.

Regulatory Environment

- Regulated by:
- URPL (drug registration, safety)
- Ministry of Health (pricing, reimbursement)
- CeZ (digital infrastructure, eRx, patient portals)
- INN prescribing mandatory.
- OTC online sales legal under verified eCommerce licenses.

Strategic Considerations

- Prioritize urban ePharmacy channels + mobile fulfilment.
- Partner with NFZ-compliant chains to access formulary traffic.
- Develop subscription-based wellness OTCs + pharmacist training support.

South Africa – Pharmaceutical Retail Market Summary (2025)

Market Size & Growth

- Total pharmaceutical retail market (2024): $3.1B
- Generics account for ~65% of retail prescriptions by volume, ~35–40% by value
- Generic retail segment size (2025 est.): ZAR 21–23B (~$1.1B–$1.2B)
- CAGR (2025–2029): ~5.3%, driven by chronic disease burden and price regulation

Market Structure

- Dominated by chains like Clicks, Dis-Chem, Medirite
- Mix of chain + independent pharmacies (~3,000 retail outlets)
- Local production by Aspen, Adcock Ingram, Cipla Medpro

eCommerce Segment

- ePharmacy OTC market (2025): $85M
- ePharmacy CAGR: ~14%, supported by private sector tech adoption
- Rx fulfillment permitted through certified e-script platforms with pharmacist validation

OTC Segment

- OTC generics dominate pain, allergy, digestive, flu/cold categories
- OTC segment size (2025 est.): $930M
- Growing popularity of nutraceuticals and traditional-herbal OTCs

Market Dynamics

- Government promotes generics through Essential Medicines List (EML) and tender pricing
- Retail generics sold both cash-based and via medical schemes
- Public-private divergence: public sector ~90% generics, private sector ~50–60%

Consumer Behaviour

- High price sensitivity; generics preferred for affordability
- Trust in chain pharmacists for substitution and guidance
- Urban adoption of digital and telepharmacy platforms increasing

Key Drivers

- Chronic disease load (e.g., hypertension, diabetes, HIV/AIDS)
- National Health Insurance (NHI) pilot programs encourage standardized generic use
- Digital access and eScript adoption expanding in metros

Key Challenges

- Inequitable pharmacy access in rural areas
- Pricing pressure under SEP (Single Exit Price) regulation
- ePharmacy regulatory framework still developing for controlled substances

Opportunities for New Entrants

- Launch of branded generics + chronic bundles via pharmacy chains
- Expansion into telehealth-integrated ePharmacy delivery models
- Partnerships with rural dispensing practices + nurse-led clinics

Regulatory Environment

- Governed by:
- South African Health Products Regulatory Authority (SAHPRA)
- SAPC (Pharmacy Council)
- Essential Drugs Programme – Dept. of Health
- SEP pricing applies to all retail drugs
- Rx ePharmacy requires: eScript + pharmacist validation

Strategic Considerations

- Align with EML + SEP compliance
- Build eCommerce OTC + Rx chronic portfolios
- Collaborate with Clicks/Dis-Chem/Medirite for national distribution

Madagascar – Pharmaceutical Retail Market Summary (2025)

Market Size & Growth

- No official 2025 market size or generics segment data published
- However, WHO confirms that over 85% of all pharmaceuticals consumed in Madagascar are generics, mostly imported
- Total pharmaceutical expenditure per capita (2022): ~$8

Market Structure

- Highly fragmented retail market dominated by:
- Independent pharmacies
- Informal outlets (drug vendors, general stores)
- No large pharmacy chains present
- Imports dominate, mainly from India, China, and France

eCommerce Segment

- No regulated ePharmacy infrastructure exists in 2025
- No official e-prescription systems implemented nationally

OTC Segment

- OTC generics widely used, particularly for:
- Malaria, fever, gastrointestinal, and pain
- No official segmentation of OTC retail value or units sold
- Products often sold through both pharmacies and informal channels

Market Dynamics

- High out-of-pocket spending (>90%)
- Dominance of generic imports, limited domestic manufacturing capacity
- Essential Medicines List (EML) governs procurement in public facilities

Consumer Behaviour

- Price sensitivity is extremely high
- High reliance on pharmacists and informal vendors for treatment advice
- Brand loyalty is low; availability and affordability drive decisions

Key Drivers

- Essential Medicines Program (EML) and donor-funded supply programs
- Support from Global Fund and GAVI for key categories (e.g., antimalarials, antibiotics)
- Population growth and urbanization slowly increasing private pharmacy demand

Key Challenges

- Unregulated informal medicine markets
- Weak pharmaceutical regulation enforcement (DPLMT)
- No national eHealth or prescription digitization system in place

Opportunities for New Entrants

- Partnerships with nonprofit distributors and urban pharmacy networks
- Introduction of branded generics for urban middle-income consumers
- Mobile health integration for prescription tracking + refill logistics

Regulatory Environment

- Regulated by:
- DPLMT (Direction de la Pharmacie, du Laboratoire et de la Médecine Traditionnelle)
- Under Ministry of Public Health Madagascar
- WHO confirms no national policy for ePharmacy or digital Rx as of 2024

Strategic Considerations

- Focus on EML-aligned generic categories (malaria, antibiotics, antipyretics)
- Navigate complex import licensing system with local agents
- Prioritize low-cost, stable shelf-life formulations for rural and informal markets

Lithuania – Pharmaceutical Retail Market Summary (2025)

Market Size & Growth

- Total retail pharmaceutical market (2022): ~€891M
- Estimated 2025 size (based on verified CAGR ~3–4%): ~€980M–€1.0B
- Generics represent ~70% of reimbursed prescription volume
- Exact 2025 generics market value not published: likely ~€320–350M based on reimbursement structure and historical shares

Market Structure

- Dominated by national pharmacy chains: Eurovaistinė (Euroapotheca), Gintarinė, BENU
- Local manufacturers: Sanitas (Valeant), Aconitum
- Pharmacies are concentrated in urban areas; rural access gaps persist

eCommerce Segment

- 100% national ePrescription adoption since 2020
- OTC sales online are legal via certified ePharmacies (e.g., eurovaistine.lt)
- Rx eCommerce requires eID + pharmacist validation

OTC Segment

- High per capita OTC use, especially in pain, flu, digestive, and supplement categories
- 2025 OTC retail estimate: ~€350M, including branded and generic products

Market Dynamics

- Reimbursement policy incentivizes INN prescribing and generic substitution
- eHealth infrastructure is fully integrated with prescription and pharmacy systems
- Out-of-pocket payments still account for ~30% of pharmaceutical expenditure

Consumer Behaviour

- High price sensitivity, especially among elderly populations
- Substitution decisions are often pharmacist-led
- Growing interest in local and herbal generics

Key Drivers

- Mandatory INN-based reimbursement model
- Strong digital infrastructure (eRx, patient portals)
- Population aging: ~21% of Lithuanians aged 65+

Key Challenges

- Retail price controls limit pharmacy margins
- Unequal access in rural municipalities
- Logistical gaps affect cold-chain-dependent generics in remote areas

Opportunities for New Entrants

- Expansion in chronic generics portfolios via NF reimbursement alignment
- Urban ePharmacy growth, especially in OTC wellness and chronic care
- Chain-led private-label generics in collaboration with Eurovaistinė or Gintarinė

Regulatory Environment

- Regulated by:
- VVKT – State Medicines Control Agency
- SAM – Ministry of Health
- VLK – Health Insurance Fund
- INN prescribing is mandatory for reimbursed medications
- Online Rx: Only through eID and certified pharmacist process

Strategic Considerations

- Align product offerings with VLK reimbursement lists
- Target expansion via urban ePharmacy + chronic bundle programs
- Build partnerships with major retail chains for private-label generics

Philippines – Pharmaceutical Retail Market Summary (2025)

Market Size & Growth

- Total retail pharma market (2024): $4.6B)
- Generics account for ~65% of prescription volume, ~45% of market value.
- Generic retail segment (2025 est.): ~ 115B ($2.0B)
- CAGR (2025–2029): ~5.7%, driven by universal healthcare rollout and substitution policies.

Market Structure

- Mix of independent drugstores (Mercury Drug, South Star) and modern pharmacy chains (Generika, Watsons).
- Rural access limited; generics penetration is higher in urban low-income segments.
- Domestic firms (Unilab Generics, RiteMed) dominate low-cost Rx/OTC space.

eCommerce Segment

- Online pharmaceutical sales (2025 est.): 9.2B (~$165M)
- Generics-focused ePharmacies (e.g., MedExpress, Generika Online) expanding.
- eCommerce share: ~3.5–4% of total retail pharma, with CAGR ~14% to 2029.

OTC Segment

- OTC generics make up $1.3B–$1.4B)** in 2024–2025.
- Popular categories: antipyretics, antihistamines, multivitamins, GI medications.
- Demand for herbal and branded generics rising.

Market Dynamics

- Post-pandemic rebound led to +12% market growth in 2023, sustained into 2024.
- DOH and PhilHealth now mandate generic substitution for public drug reimbursement.
- Prescription drug costs remain out-of-pocket for ~60% of population.

Consumer Behaviour

- Price sensitivity is high; over 70% of consumers opt for generics when available.
- Trust in community pharmacists and drugstore loyalty is strong.
- Urban Gen Z segments shifting to online purchases of supplements and OTCs.

Key Drivers

- Universal Health Care Law (RA 11223) enforcement expands retail demand.
- Public procurement favors low-cost generic manufacturers.
- Increasing NCD burden (hypertension, diabetes) drives chronic Rx generics.
- Fast-growing middle class adopting preventive OTC regimens.

Key Challenges

- Fragmented retail market with price variability and counterfeit concerns.
- Low digital prescription adoption limits ePharmacy scale.
- Infrastructure gaps in rural provinces and islands hamper distribution.

Opportunities for New Entrants

- Generic ePharmacy platforms for urban users.
- Bundled services (Rx + OTC + diagnostics) for clinic-pharmacy partnerships.
- Private-label generics through major pharmacy chains.

Regulatory Environment

- Overseen by FDA Philippines (under DOH); importers must register under CPR (Certificate of Product Registration).
- Generics Act (RA 6675) mandates generic prescribing for all physicians.
- IRP and price ceilings applied to 132 essential generics as of 2024.
- ePharmacy regulation under DOH & DICT with developing e-prescription laws.

Strategic Considerations

- Position generics as affordable, pharmacist-recommended alternatives.
- Partner with PhilHealth-accredited drug outlets for reimbursement capture.
- Leverage logistics and POS digitization for scale and compliance.

JAPAN – PHARMACEUTICAL RETAIL MARKET SUMMARY (2025)

Market Size & Growth

- Total retail pharma (2024): $78B)
- Generics share: ~80% by volume, ~45% by value
- Generic retail size (2025 est.): $32B)
- CAGR (2025–2029): ~3.8%

Market Structure

- Led by drugstore chains (Matsumoto Kiyoshi, Welcia)
- Key local suppliers: Sawai, Nichi-Iko, Towa
- Regional consolidation is rising

eCommerce Segment

- ePharmacy (2025): $1.5B)**; ~2% of retail pharma
- OTC mail-order growth at ~11% CAGR
- Limited by strict ePharmacy rules (Rx not allowed)

OTC Segment

- OTC generics = $3.8B)**
- Focus: analgesics, antihistamines, GI meds, supplements

Market Dynamics

- Government-mandated substitution & NHI pressure
- Regular price cuts squeeze margins
- Aging drives chronic disease-related demand

Consumer Behaviour

- Trust in local generics
- Digital OTC growing among 30–50s
- Pharmacists act as advisors but face capacity limits

Key Drivers

- NHI policy targeting >80% generic Rx rate
- Aging (29% aged 65+)
- Digital Rx & refill pilots expanding

Key Challenges

- Frequent price revisions
- ePharmacy constraints
- Pharmacist shortages
- Brand skepticism for foreign generics

Opportunities

- NHI-aligned generics
- Mail-order OTC wellness (e.g., sleep, gut)
- Regional chain partnerships

Regulatory Environment

- Overseen by MHLW/PMDA
- Only OTC (Type 1–3) allowed online
- Price revision: every 2 years (April)

Strategy

- Focus on NHI pricing, aging-targeted SKUs
- Leverage digital refill models + urban eCommerce
- Align with 2026–27 eRx rollout

Italy – Pharmaceutical Retail Market Summary (2025)

Market Size & Growth

- Total retail pharma (2024): ~€24.2B
- Generics: ~38% by volume, ~26% by value
- Generic retail market (2025 est.): ~€6.3B, with CAGR ~3.5% (2025–2029)

Market Structure

- Dominated by pharmacy chains + independent outlets
- Key players: Teva Italia, EG, DOC Generici
- Growth in co-branded private-label generics by retail chains

eCommerce Segment

- OTC ePharmacy (2025): ~€380M, ~5% of retail OTC
- ePharmacy CAGR: ~13%, led by wellness, supplements
- Rx eCommerce restricted to "click-and-collect"

OTC Segment

- OTC generics (2025 est.): ~€2.2B
- High-volume products: pain relievers, antacids, supplements
- Parapharmaceuticals (non-Rx health) gaining market share

Market Dynamics

- Government price negotiations keep margins tight
- Aging population drives demand for low-cost chronic meds
- COVID-accelerated ePharmacy usage sustaining momentum

Consumer Behaviour

- Price-aware but brand-trusting
- Uptake of generics is higher in northern and urban regions
- OTC and supplement online buying growing among 30–60s

Key Drivers

- Cost-saving policies under SSN (National Health Service)
- Support for biosimilars and generic substitutions
- Rising prevalence of lifestyle diseases

Key Challenges

- Regulatory price caps and discounting pressures
- Pharmacist gatekeeping slows generic substitution
- Fragmented digital Rx infrastructure

Opportunities

- Retail-branded OTC generics
- ePharmacy integration with telemedicine
- Distribution partnerships in aging-heavy rural regions

Regulatory Environment

- Regulated by AIFA (Agenzia Italiana del Farmaco)
- Mandatory prescription by INN for public reimbursements
- OTCs allowed online; Rx delivery prohibited

Strategy

- Align with AIFA reimbursement lists
- Invest in ePharmacy + pharmacist-led digital support
- Focus on OTC wellness + chronic condition SKUs

Malaysia – Pharmaceutical Retail Market Summary (2025)

Market Size & Growth

- Retail pharmaceutical market (2024): ~RM 10.5B (~$2.2B). Generics account for ~60–65% of units sold.
- Generic retail segment estimated at ~RM 5.8B ($1.2B) in 2025.
- Forecast CAGR (2025–2029): 6.2%, driven by government procurement policy, aging population, and increased chronic disease prevalence.

Market Structure

- Dual-layered retail: chain pharmacies (e.g., Watsons, Guardian) + independent outlets.
- Urban regions dominated by chains; rural areas served by general trade and licensed pharmacists.
- Local manufacturers (Duopharma, Pharmaniaga) hold strong generics share.

eCommerce Segment

- ePharmacy segment valued at ~RM 500M ($106M) in 2024, projected CAGR ~12.5% through 2029.
- Growth drivers: MySejahtera-linked health data, expanding logistics, and wellness-oriented OTC uptake.

OTC Segment

- OTC generics = ~40% of total generics retail sales.
- Top categories: analgesics, vitamins, antihistamines, and digestive aids.
- Increasing demand for natural and halal-certified products.

Market Dynamics

- Skim Perubatan Madani (SPM) encourages substitution with generics in private retail.
- Public-private integration: many patients fill prescriptions in private pharmacies using public coverage.
- Generic substitution incentivized via bulk procurement programs (APPL Scheme).

Consumer Behaviour

- Cost remains primary driver – >65% of consumers actively seek lower-priced alternatives.
- High trust in community pharmacists for OTC and minor ailment advice.
- Rise in online wellness and supplement shopping among urban Gen Z and millennial users.

Key Drivers

- Government bulk tenders favoring generics
- Demographic shift toward chronic NCDs
- Digital infrastructure: national eHealth rollout supports Rx-tracking and cross-dispensary data
- Export restrictions on originators from key markets increased generic substitution

Key Challenges

- Heavy price controls (Reference Pricing Model) limit retail margin on essential generics
- Parallel imports and counterfeit risks affect consumer trust online
- Fragmentation between public and private sector hinders supply chain efficiency

Opportunities for New Entrants

- ePharmacy platforms targeting health-conscious urban middle class
- Halal-certified, plant-based generics and functional OTCs
- Regional expansion via partnerships with local wholesalers and clinics

Regulatory Environment

- Regulated by NPRA under Ministry of Health (Malaysia).
- Product Registration Holder (PRH) model required for foreign entrants.
- OTC classified under Category X; online Rx requires licensed pharmacist oversight.
- Halal certification for pharmaceuticals gaining official regulatory pathways via JAKIM.

Strategic Considerations

- Align with national formulary (Generic Medicines List) and e-prescription rollout.
- Partner with retail chains for last-mile delivery and wellness bundling.
- Position for regional export via ASEAN harmonization (AMRH, MRA compliance).

Ukraine – Pharmaceutical Retail Market Summary (2025)

Market Size & Growth

- Retail market size: ~$2.7B (2024), with generics accounting for ~70% by volume, ~47% by value.
- CAGR (2025–2029): ~5.4% for generics.
- OTC market: ~$1.45B, growing at ~4% annually.
- Retail prescription generics: ~$340–400M, relatively stable.

Market Structure

- Highly fragmented: Around 10,000 outlets.
- Urban chains (e.g., ANC, Dobroho Dnia) dominate; rural areas underserved.
- Local players (Farmak, Darnitsa) lead generic supply.

eCommerce Segment

- Legal since 2023; OTC ePharmacy sales ~ $53M (2025), ~1.9% of OTC market.
- CAGR: ~13% (2025–2029), driven by mobile access and urban demand.

OTC Segment

- OTC generics make up ~35% of retail volume.
- Key categories: analgesics (~$460M), vitamins, flu/cold, GI meds.
- Herbal/supplements rising in popularity.

Market Dynamics

- Strong rebound post-2022: +18–20% growth in UAH, ~9% in USD (2024).
- Generic substitution and import substitution programs expanding.
- Pharmacists act as key retail advisors.

Consumer Behaviour

- >75% out-of-pocket purchases; highly price-sensitive.
- Strong trust in pharmacists; interest in natural/OTC wellness products increasing.

Key Drivers

- Chronic disease prevalence and population aging.
- Reimbursement register (>300 INNs) and digital prescribing (eRx ~50% adoption).
- Urban growth in mobile-first pharmacy models.

Key Challenges

- Import dependency, FX volatility, and supply chain disruptions.
- Regulatory burden: price controls, IP, and reimbursement complexity.
- Limited infrastructure in rural areas.

Opportunities for New Entrants

- Private-label OTCs, affordable generics.
- Urban ePharmacy and telepharmacy platforms.
- Logistics/distribution models targeting rural recovery zones.

Regulatory Environment

- Regulated by State Service on Medicines (MoH).
- ePrescription mandatory since 2019; 50% adoption.
- IRP (International Reference Pricing) expected to expand to OTC by late 2025.

Strategic Considerations

- Focus on price-accessible generics and pharmacy-aligned distribution.
- Partner with trusted chains; integrate digital Rx/payment systems.
- Build resilient supply chains aligned with evolving policy.

Singapore – Pharmaceutical Retail Market Summary (2025)

Market Size & Growth

- Total Retail Pharmacy Market: US$6.16 billion in 2025, projected CAGR of 4.45% through 2029.
- OTC Market: Expected to reach US$1.22 billion in 2025, with 5.29% CAGR (2025–2029).
- Prescription Drugs: Forecast to hit US$1.80 billion in 2025, growing at 3.81% CAGR.

Market Structure

- Retail Formats: Combination of large chains (e.g., Watsons with more than 100 stores), supermarket pharmacies (NTUC FairPrice), and many independent pharmacies.
- Urban Focus: High pharmacy density in urban districts, with chains evenly distributed for convenience.

eCommerce Segment

- Online OTC Sales: US$60.5 million in 2025, accounting for ≈14% of OTC revenue.
- Health eCommerce: Projected US$188 million in 2025, comprising 28.4% of care eCommerce.
- Drivers: Tech-savvy population and demand for convenience.

OTC Segment

- Key Categories: Cold & cough (US$304 M), analgesics; total OTC ≈US$1.22 bn.
- Growth Drivers: Aging population (19% aged 65+ by 2030), self-medication trend, and preventive health focus.

Market Dynamics

- Generic Uptake: Growing availability of generics encouraged by HSA regulatory support.
- Convenience Culture: Pharmacies located in supermarkets and urban hotspots support impulse and repeat OTC purchases.
- Product Trust: High healthcare standards drive consumer confidence.

Consumer Behaviour

- Price-conscious but quality-focused consumers; willingness to pay for trusted generic alternatives.
- Pharmacies (e.g. Watsons, Unity, FairPrice) are both retail and advisory hubs.

Key Drivers

- Chronic Disease Rise: Increased demand for maintenance drugs.
- Digital Integration: Online pharmacy and e-prescription services expanding.
- Government Support: Policy support for generic drug production and retail modernization.

Key Challenges

- Competition: High saturation in retail chains; margin pressures.
- Regulatory Scrutiny: Strict quality and safety standards set by HSA.
- Pricing Pressure: Balancing affordability with profitability under price-sensitive market.

Opportunities

- Modern Retail Expansion: Enhancing omnichannel experiences via click-and-collect.
- Generic & Wellness Products: Strengthening private-label generics and OTC health supplements.
- E-Pharmacy Innovation: Leveraging existing eCommerce infrastructure to scale delivery services.

Regulatory Environment

- Key Authority: Health Sciences Authority (HSA) regulates drug approvals.
- Standards: Strict GMP, bioequivalence, and labelling rules; price controls limited mainly to public-health programs.
- Supportive Ecosystem: Infrastructure encourages local R&D and generic entrants.

Strategic Considerations

- Focus on trusted generic solutions supported by HSA endorsements.
- Develop hybrid retail models combining physical locations with online presence.
- Expand private-label and wellness ranges to complement generics.
- Collaborate with major chains and supermarkets for wider distribution and brand reach.

Armenia – Pharmaceutical Retail Market Summary (2025)

Market Size & Growth

- Retail Pharmaceutical Market projected at USD 267.8 million in 2025.
- OTC market expected to reach USD 177.9 million, growing at 8.34% CAGR (2025–2029).
- Prescription drug retail: USD 148.6 million, 5.53% CAGR.

Market Structure

- Dominated by chains like AlfaPharm (~170 outlets) and Natali Pharm (~100).
- Urban-centric distribution; rural areas remain underserved.

eCommerce Segment

- ePharmacy sales: USD 0.4 million in 2025; 42.4% of Armenia's health eCommerce.
- Growth driven by internet access and urban consumer convenience.

OTC Segment

- High demand for pain relief, cold & flu, and digestive products.
- Self-medication trend accelerating OTC growth.

Market Dynamics

- Market heavily import-dependent, making it vulnerable to currency and supply shocks.
- Strict regulatory oversight ensures product safety and efficacy.
- Pricing controls applied to essential public medicines via external reference pricing.

Consumer Behaviour

- Highly price-sensitive consumers prefer affordable generics.
- Pharmacist recommendation still plays a traditional but key role in OTC purchases.

Key Drivers

- Government identifies pharma as a strategic priority.
- Ongoing healthcare reforms are improving access and affordability.

Key Challenges

- Small market size limits large-scale investment.
- High out-of-pocket spending tied to economic stability.

Opportunities for New Entrants

- Scope to expand affordable generics to meet rising demand.
- ePharmacy has strong growth potential in cities.

Regulatory Environment

- All drugs must be registered by the Ministry of Health.
- Pricing caps applied to selected publicly financed medicines.

Strategic Considerations

- Prioritize generic portfolios with strong urban reach.
- Invest in digital retail and build local partnerships with dominant chains.

Sri Lanka – Pharmaceutical Retail Market Summary (2025)

Market Size & Growth

- Estimated retail market value: USD 750 million in 2025.
- Generics dominate ~65% of total volume.
- Expected CAGR: 4.1% (2025–2030).
- Retail pharmacies contribute over 80% of total pharmaceutical sales.

Market Structure

- Dominated by independent pharmacies; urban-heavy distribution.
- Product mix includes high-volume generics for chronic care; branded drugs for acute conditions.

eCommerce Segment

- Small but growing (under 7.1% share).
- Limited by digital infrastructure and regulatory gaps.
- Urban youth driving adoption.

OTC Segment

- Valued at USD 150–180 million in 2025.
- Demand driven by self-medication and awareness campaigns.

Market Dynamics & Consumer Behavior

- Price-sensitive consumers prefer affordable generics.
- Pharmacist recommendations are highly influential.
- Urbanization and chronic disease prevalence are key demand drivers.

Key Challenges

- Supply chain disruptions.
- Regulatory complexities.
- Prevalence of counterfeit medicines.

Opportunities for New Entrants

- Affordable, high-quality generic brands.
- Partnerships with local pharmacies and DTP distribution models.
- Consumer and pharmacist education to build trust and loyalty.

Regulatory Environment

- Regulated by NMRA with strict guidelines on pricing and product approvals.
- Emphasis on quality assurance and bioequivalence.

Strategic Considerations

- Focus on reliable distribution and pharmacist engagement.
- Strong local presence and regulatory compliance are essential.
- Consumer education can accelerate brand penetration and loyalty.

Sudan – Pharmaceutical Retail Market Summary (2025)

Market Size & Growth

- Market Value (2025): Estimated at USD 350–400 million, with 65%+ share from generics.
- Growth Rate: CAGR 4.5–5.5% through 2030, fueled by rising demand for affordable drugs and pharmacy expansion.

Market Structure

- Retail Focus: Dominated by independent urban pharmacies; rural areas underserved.
- Product Mix: Generics preferred for chronic care; branded drugs for acute conditions.

eCommerce Segment

- Share: <1%, but growing.
- Barriers: Weak digital infrastructure and regulatory uncertainty.
- Potential: Young urban consumers driving future adoption.

OTC Segment

- Market Size (2025): USD 100–120 million.
- Trends: Strong growth in pain relief, cold remedies, and digestion-related products.

Market Dynamics

- Drivers: Price sensitivity, pharmacist trust, chronic disease growth.
- Inventory: Fast turnover of essentials in cities; irregular supply elsewhere.

Consumer Behavior

- Influence: Pharmacists play a major advisory role.
- Preferences: Affordability, accessibility, and local trust matter most.

Key Drivers

- Urbanization, NCD rise, and health awareness improving retail demand.

Key Challenges

- Supply chain instability, complex regulations, and counterfeit drugs.

Opportunities for Entrants

- High demand for low-cost generics.
- Local partnerships with pharmacy chains and wholesalers.
- Direct-to-pharmacy (DTP) distribution can improve efficiency and margins.

Regulatory Landscape

- Authority: National Medicines and Poisons Board (NMPB).
- Rules: Strict retail pharmacy licensing and generic quality standards.

Strategic Priorities

- Build reliable local distribution, engage trusted pharmacists, and invest in consumer awareness to become a recognized, affordable brand.
- Note: The recent conflicts in Sudan would significantly impact many of these points, especially supply chain, manufacturing, and distribution.

El Salvador – Pharmaceutical Retail Market Summary (2025)

Market Size & Growth

- Estimated at USD 765–800 million, with over 60% attributed to generic medicines.
- 4.8–5.2% CAGR (2025–2030), driven by increasing demand for low-cost treatments and urban pharmaceutical consumption.
- Over 85% of pharmaceutical sales occur through retail outlets, with hospitals and institutional channels accounting for the remainder.

Market Structure

- El Salvador has a relatively dense retail pharmacy network in urban areas, with growing presence in peri-urban zones.
- Retail Format: Dominated by independent pharmacies, small chains (e.g., Farmacias San Nicolás), and franchise-style outlets.
- Product Mix: Generic drugs dominate chronic illness treatment segments; branded drugs still favoured for acute care and specialized therapies.

eCommerce Segment

- Market Share: Still under 3% of pharmaceutical retail sales in 2025, but growing slowly.
- Challenges: Limited payment gateways, lack of regulatory clarity, and low digital penetration in rural zones.
- Growth Driver: Younger urban consumers prefer "click and collect" models tied to retail chains.

OTC Segment

- Retail OTC Size (2025): Estimated at USD 220–240 million, with continued strong shelf turnover in cold/flu, digestive, and pain relief categories.
- Consumer Trends: High demand for vitamins, painkillers, and herbal remedies.

Market Dynamics

- Generics are preferred in retail due to affordability and adequate therapeutic equivalence.
- Retail Trust: Pharmacists play a key advisory role; brand loyalty is pharmacist-driven.

Key Retail Drivers

- Urbanization & Middle-Class Expansion
- Growing Chronic Disease Burden

Key Retail Challenges

- Supply Chain Fragmentation: Distribution gaps delay rural restocking.
- Pharmacist Shortages: Smaller towns face professional talent gaps.
- Regulatory Burden: Complex pricing and import rules hinder new retail entrants.

Opportunities for New Retail-Focused Entrants

- Strong demand for Quality lowcost generics across urban and peri-urban areas.
- Retail Partnership Model: Collaborate with established pharmacies and local chains for distribution.
- Direct-to-Pharmacy (DTP) Models: Minimize intermediaries and maximize shelf visibility.

Regulatory Environment

- Governing Body: National Directorate of Medicines (DNM)
- Retail-Focused Regulations: Drug pricing, retail pharmacy licensing, and advertising guidelines are actively enforced.
- Bioequivalence Enforcement: Mandatory for all generic drugs since 2016—key to gaining consumer confidence.

Strategic Considerations for New Entrants

- Retail-Centric Salesforce: Building a pharmacy-level distribution team is more impactful than hospital-based reps.
- Stock Visibility Tools: Implement POS-based monitoring for restocking trends and consumer preferences.
- Consumer Outreach: Community events and health drives build strong brand associations.
- Localized Pricing Strategy: Tiered pricing can improve access and brand penetration.

Paraguay – Pharmaceutical Retail Market Summary (2025)

Market Snapshot

- Paraguay's retail pharmaceutical market is valued at approximately USD 380 million (2024–25), with a projected CAGR of 6.5–7% through 2030.
- Growth is fueled by economic expansion, rising chronic disease burden, and increasing urban demand.
- The market is highly genericized—local manufacturers supply ~70% of drug units (mainly generics and OTCs), though ~60% of value is still tied to branded imports.

Market Structure

- 2,400+ licensed pharmacies, dominated by chains in urban centers.
- Local manufacturing covers routine generics; imports supply high-cost brands.
- Retail market is fragmented but urban areas see high concentration of sales (>58% from Asunción/Central).
- Chain pharmacies captured >90% of sales in Asunción by 2014 and continue to grow.

eCommerce Segment

- ePharmacy valued at ~USD 2.7M (2025), <9% of retail share, but growing at 8.5% CAGR.
- Still early-stage; opportunity exists in home delivery, telehealth integration, and online brand differentiation.

OTC Segment

- OTC market driven by preventive health and self-medication trends.
- Fast growth in vitamins, pain relief, herbal remedies.
- High cross-border OTC smuggling from Argentina erodes official sales.

Key Drivers

- High out-of-pocket spending (~36% of health expenditure), making pharmacies key health access points.
- Increasing prevalence of chronic conditions (hypertension, diabetes, obesity).
- Urbanization and digital adoption support retail and eHealth expansion.

Key Challenges

- Regulatory complexity: DINAVISA requires lengthy product registrations and restricts Rx advertising.
- Strict price controls: Fixed pharmacy markups and new OTC reference pricing squeeze margins.

- Informal markets: Border smuggling and informal OTC channels distort pricing and undermine regulation.
- Geographic disparity: Rural regions lack access, logistics are weak outside Asunción.

Opportunities for New Entrants

- Affordable generics and branded substitutes in NCDs, biosimilars, and OTC.
- Rural expansion via franchise or mobile pharmacy models.
- Digital-first retail models: eCommerce, telepharmacy, influencer-led OTC marketing.
- Partnerships with local players (CIFARMA members) for regulatory ease and manufacturing.

Regulatory Outlook

- DINAVISA oversees all market access, with evolving frameworks (e.g., 2024 OTC price reform).
- No reimbursement system – pricing must suit direct consumer purchases.
- Strict controls on marketing: Rx advertising banned, OTC ads require pre-approval.

Strategic Considerations

- Partner with local distributors or manufacturers to navigate DINAVISA.
- Focus on affordability and access, especially in generics, OTC, and wellness.
- Target urban pharmacy chains for volume, and rural markets for differentiation.
- Monitor policy reforms (pricing, digital sales) and build compliance capacity early.

Morocco – Pharmaceutical Retail Market Summary (2025)

Market Size & Growth

- The pharmaceutical retail market in Morocco is experiencing robust growth, with a Compound Annual Growth Rate (CAGR) of approximately 7.5%, reaching USD 1.5 billion in sales as of Q1 2024.

Market Structure

- Distribution Channels: The market encompasses both online and offline retail segments, catering to diverse consumer preferences.
- Drug Types: Sales are distributed among generic, over-the-counter (OTC), and patented drugs, reflecting a balanced demand across categories.
- End Users: The retail market serves various segments, including drug retail, health products retail, chemical medicine retail, and medicinal materials retail.

Key Players

- Local corporations have shown significant growth, with companies like Bottu SA leading the market with a 6.2% share. Sothema is noted as the fastest-growing among the top 10, with an 11.6% growth rate.

Drivers

- Urbanization & Demographics: Rapid urban growth and a youthful population are increasing demand for accessible pharmaceutical products.
- Healthcare Reforms: Government initiatives aimed at expanding healthcare coverage are bolstering the pharmaceutical retail sector.
- Digital Transformation: The rise of e-commerce platforms is facilitating online pharmaceutical sales, enhancing market reach.

Challenges

- Regulatory Compliance: Navigating the regulatory landscape requires thorough understanding and adherence to local guidelines.
- Infrastructure Limitations: Challenges in supply chain logistics and limited infrastructure in rural areas can impact market expansion.
- Counterfeit Medicines: The presence of counterfeit drugs in the market poses risks to consumer safety and brand integrity.

Strategic Recommendations

- Local Partnerships: Collaborate with established local distributors and pharmacy chains to leverage existing networks.
- Digital Engagement: Invest in e-commerce platforms and digital marketing to reach a broader customer base.
- Regulatory Navigation: Engage with local regulatory bodies to ensure compliance and facilitate efficient market entry.
- Quality Assurance: Implement stringent quality control measures to build consumer trust and combat counterfeit products.

Ecuador – Pharmaceutical Retail Market Summary (2025)

Market Size & Growth

- Total Pharmaceutical Market: The pharmaceutical market in Ecuador is estimated to reach USD 2.95 billion in 2025, with a projected annual growth rate (CAGR 2025-2035) of 5.5%, leading to a market volume of USD 5.23 billion by 2035.
- Over-the-Counter (OTC) Pharmaceuticals: The OTC pharmaceuticals market is projected to generate USD 460 million in 2025, with an estimated CAGR (2025-2035) of 5.5%, reaching USD 820 million by 2035.
- Prescription Drugs: The prescription drugs market is estimated to account for the remaining portion of the total market, approximately USD 2.49 billion in 2025. While a specific CAGR for this segment alone wasn't previously detailed, it is expected to contribute to the overall market growth of 5.5%.

eCommerce Segment

- Pharmaceuticals eCommerce: The pharmaceuticals eCommerce market is expected to show growth from the USD 28.2 million projected for 2024, reflecting increasing online adoption. The previously noted CAGR of 7.7% (2024-2028) suggests continued expansion.
- OTC Drugs eCommerce: The OTC drugs eCommerce market is expected to show growth from the USD 7.1 million projected for 2024, with a previously noted CAGR of 8.0% (2024-2028) indicating further expansion in 2025.
- Prescription Drugs eCommerce: The prescription drugs eCommerce market is expected to show growth from the USD 20.3 million projected for 2024, with a previously noted CAGR of 7.7% (2024-2028) suggesting continued growth into 2025.

Market Dynamics

- Consumer Behavior: There is a growing preference for self-medication and convenient access to healthcare products, driving the demand for OTC pharmaceuticals.

Product Segmentation

- OTC Drugs: Significant growth due to rising self-medication trends.
- Prescription Drugs: Continued demand, especially for chronic disease management.

Distribution Channels

- Retail Pharmacies: Remain dominant in the pharmaceutical retail market.
- Online Pharmacies: Increasing presence, particularly in the OTC segment.

Regulatory Environment

- Regulatory Bodies: Oversight by the National Agency for Regulation, Control, and Sanitary Surveillance (ARCSA).

- Market Access: Regulations are in place for drug registration, pricing, and distribution; however, navigating these can be complex for new entrants.

Strategic Considerations

- Market Entry: Opportunities exist for both local and international companies, particularly in the OTC and eCommerce segments.
- Partnerships: Collaborations with local distributors and pharmacies can facilitate market penetration.
- Consumer Education: Investing in consumer awareness campaigns can drive demand for OTC products.

Uganda's – Pharmaceutical Retail Market Summary (2025)

Market Size & Growth

- The pharmaceutical retail market in Uganda is experiencing steady growth, driven by increasing healthcare demands, population expansion, and rising awareness about healthcare and treatment options.
- While there's no official CAGR (Compound Annual Growth Rate) for Uganda's pharmaceutical retail market in most available public data is primarily due to the limited transparency and underdeveloped data reporting mechanisms in the Ugandan pharmaceutical sector. Based on regional growth trends (Kenya: ~7–9%, Ghana: ~7–8%) and Uganda's stable but modest economic expansion (GDP growth avg. ~5.3%), the estimated CAGR is between 6.5% - 8.5%.

Market Structure

- Distribution Channels: The market encompasses both online and offline retail segments, catering to diverse consumer preferences.
- Drug Types: Sales are distributed among generic, over-the-counter (OTC), and patented drugs, reflecting a balanced demand across categories.
- End Users: The retail market serves various segments, including drug retail, health products retail, chemical medicine retail, and medicinal materials retail.

E-Pharmacy Growth

- The pharmaceuticals eCommerce market in Uganda is predicted to reach USD 1.2 million by 2025, accounting for 45.9% of the Health Care eCommerce market in the country. It is expected to increase over the next years, with a projected market volume of USD 2.4 million by 2029.

Key Drivers

- Healthcare Accessibility: Challenges in the public healthcare system have led consumers to rely more on pharmacies for timely access to medications.
- Economic Factors: Economic development and population growth are increasing the demand for pharmaceutical products.
- Digital Adoption: Increased internet penetration and smartphone usage have facilitated the growth of online pharmacy services.

Challenges

- Regulatory Environment: Navigating the regulatory landscape requires compliance with local guidelines, which can be complex for new entrants.
- Supply Chain Issues: Economic fluctuations can impact the availability and pricing of pharmaceutical products.

Strategic Recommendations

- Local Partnerships: Collaborate with established local pharmacies and distributors to leverage existing networks and market knowledge.
- Digital Integration: Invest in e-commerce platforms and digital marketing to reach a broader customer base and enhance service offerings.
- Regulatory Compliance: Engage with local regulatory bodies to ensure compliance and facilitate efficient market entry.
- Product Diversification: Expand product lines to include high-demand OTC and wellness products to cater to evolving consumer preferences.

Myanmar – Pharmaceutical Retail Market Summary (2025)

Market Size & Growth

- The pharmaceutical retail market in Myanmar is projected to reach approximately USD 1.1 billion by 2030, growing at a Compound Annual Growth Rate (CAGR) of 7.4% from 2024.

Market Structure

- Retail Outlets: There are approximately 10,000 retail outlets selling both allopathic and traditional medicines across the country.
- Urban Concentration: Over 60% of drug sales occur in the major cities of Yangon and Mandalay.
- Traditional vs. Modern Trade: The retail sector is predominantly traditional, with 90% of the industry still dominated by traditional trade methods.

Online Retail Segment

- The pharmaceuticals eCommerce market in Myanmar is expected to reach USD 23.2 million by 2025, reflecting a 16% growth compared to 2024.
- The online share of the pharmaceutical retail market is currently 13.8% and is projected to increase to 16.8% by 2029.

Key Drivers

- Healthcare Awareness: Increasing health consciousness among the population is driving demand for pharmaceutical products.
- Urbanization: Rapid urban growth is contributing to the expansion of retail pharmacies in urban centres.
- Digital Adoption: The rise of e-commerce platforms is facilitating access to pharmaceutical products, especially in urban areas.

Challenges

- Regulatory Compliance: Navigating the regulatory landscape requires thorough understanding and adherence to local guidelines.
- Infrastructure Limitations: Challenges in supply chain logistics and limited infrastructure in rural areas can impact market expansion.
- Counterfeit Medicines: The presence of counterfeit drugs in the market poses risks to consumer safety and brand integrity.

Strategic Recommendations

- Local Partnerships: Collaborate with established local distributors and pharmacy chains to leverage existing networks.
- Digital Engagement: Invest in e-commerce platforms and digital marketing to reach a broader customer base.
- Regulatory Navigation: Engage with local regulatory bodies to ensure compliance and facilitate efficient market entry.
- Quality Assurance: Implement stringent quality control measures to build consumer trust and combat counterfeit products.

Argentina – Pharmaceutical Retail Market Summary (2025)

Market Size & Growth

- The pharmaceutical retail market in Argentina was valued at approximately USD 4.88 billion in 2024 and is projected to reach USD 8.6 billion by 2030, growing at a Compound Annual Growth Rate (CAGR) of 9.9% from 2025 to 2030.

Market Structure

- Prescription vs. OTC: Prescription drugs dominate the market, but Over-The-Counter (OTC) products are the fastest-growing segment, driven by self-medication trends and increased health awareness.
- Retail Channels: The market comprises a mix of independent pharmacies and chain drugstores, with Farmacity being a notable player operating across multiple provinces.
- E-Pharmacy Growth: The e-pharmacy sector is expanding rapidly, with a projected CAGR of over 14.89% from 2023 to 2028, offering services like online consultations and home deliveries.

Key Drivers

- Healthcare Accessibility: Challenges in the public healthcare system, such as long waiting times, have led consumers to rely more on pharmacies for timely access to medications.
- Economic Factors: Economic instability and inflation have increased the demand for affordable generic medications, influencing purchasing behaviors.
- Digital Adoption: Increased internet penetration and smartphone usage have facilitated the growth of online pharmacy services.

Challenges

- Regulatory Environment: Navigating the regulatory landscape requires compliance with local guidelines, which can be complex for new entrants.
- Supply Chain Issues: Economic fluctuations can impact the availability and pricing of pharmaceutical products.

Strategic Recommendations

- Local Partnerships: Collaborate with established local pharmacies and distributors to leverage existing networks and market knowledge.
- Digital Integration: Invest in e-commerce platforms and digital marketing to reach a broader customer base and enhance service offerings.
- Regulatory Compliance: Engage with local regulatory bodies to ensure compliance and facilitate efficient market entry.
- Product Diversification: Expand product lines to include high-demand OTC and wellness products to cater to evolving consumer preferences.

Egypt – Pharmaceutical Retail Market Summary (2025)

Market Size & Growth

- The generic pharmaceutical market in Egypt was valued at approximately USD 1.28 billion in 2023 and is projected to grow at a Compound Annual Growth Rate (CAGR) of 6.07% through 2029.

Regulatory Environment

- Regulatory Authority: The Egyptian Drug Authority (EDA), established under Law No. 151 of 2019, oversees the regulation of pharmaceutical products in Egypt.
- Registration Process: The EDA has adopted Good Reliance Practices (GRelP) in line with World Health Organization (WHO) guidelines, facilitating the evaluation of safety, efficacy, and quality data for pharmaceutical products.

Market Dynamics

- Import Reliance: Egypt imported pharmaceutical products worth USD 3.52 billion in 2024, indicating a significant reliance on imports to meet domestic demand.
- Export Growth: Pharmaceutical exports reached USD 447.15 million in 2024, reflecting the country's growing capabilities in pharmaceutical manufacturing.

Opportunities

- Chronic Disease Management: The rising prevalence of chronic diseases such as diabetes and cardiovascular conditions increases demand for affordable generic medications.
- Local Manufacturing Initiatives: Government incentives aim to boost local pharmaceutical production, reducing dependency on imports and promoting self-sufficiency.

Challenges

- Regulatory Compliance: Navigating the regulatory landscape requires thorough understanding and adherence to EDA guidelines, which can be complex for new market entrants.
- Economic Factors: Currency fluctuations and inflation may impact pricing strategies and profitability for pharmaceutical companies operating in Egypt.

Strategic Recommendations

- Local Partnerships: Collaborate with Egyptian pharmaceutical firms to leverage existing infrastructure and market knowledge.
- Regulatory Navigation: Invest in regulatory expertise to ensure compliance and facilitate efficient market entry.

- Market Focus: Prioritize the development and distribution of generics for high-demand therapeutic areas, particularly chronic diseases.
- Infrastructure Investment: Support initiatives aimed at improving manufacturing and distribution capabilities within Egypt.

Ghana – Pharmaceutical Retail Market Summary (2025)

Market Size & Growth

- The pharmaceutical market is projected to reach GHS 3.96 billion (~USD 680 million) by 2025, driven by population growth, urbanization, and increased healthcare spending.

Regulatory Environment

- Regulatory Bodies: The Food and Drugs Authority (FDA) oversees drug registration and compliance, while the Pharmacy Council regulates pharmacy practice.
- Registration Process: Generic drug registration requires submission of comprehensive dossiers, including proof of Good Manufacturing Practice (GMP) compliance and bioequivalence studies.

Market Dynamics

- Import Reliance: Approximately 70% of pharmaceuticals are imported, primarily from India and China, highlighting opportunities for local production.
- Local Manufacturing: The government is promoting local manufacturing through tax incentives and the establishment of pharmaceutical funds to support domestic companies.

Opportunities

- Essential Medicines: High demand for affordable generics in areas such as antimalarials, antibiotics, and treatments for non-communicable diseases.
- E-commerce Growth: The rise of online pharmacies and digital health platforms is expanding access to medicines.

Challenges

- Regulatory Compliance: Navigating the regulatory landscape requires thorough understanding and adherence to FDA and Pharmacy Council guidelines.
- Infrastructure Limitations: Challenges in supply chain logistics and manufacturing infrastructure can impact market entry and distribution.

Strategic Recommendations

- Local Partnerships: Collaborate with Ghanaian pharmaceutical firms to leverage existing infrastructure and market knowledge.
- Regulatory Navigation: Invest in regulatory expertise to ensure compliance and facilitate efficient market entry.
- Market Focus: Prioritize the development and distribution of generics for high-demand therapeutic areas.
- Digital Engagement: Utilize digital platforms to reach a broader customer base and streamline distribution.

Kenya – Pharmaceutical Retail Market Summary (2025)

Market Potential

- The pharmaceutical market is projected to cross USD 1 billion by 2030, driven by a rising middle class, chronic diseases, and government health reforms.

Regulatory Environment

- Regulated by the Pharmacy and Poisons Board (PPB); generic drug registration requires WHO-format dossiers, GMP certification, and bioequivalence data.

Key Opportunities

- Strong government push for local manufacturing and import substitution.
- East African Community (EAC) harmonization allows regional expansion post-entry.

Challenges

- Infrastructure gaps and regulatory delays.
- Price sensitivity in both public and private sectors.

Success Factors

- Partner with local players.
- Offer WHO-prequalified generics for public tenders.
- Focus on essential medicines and NCDs (e.g., diabetes, hypertension).

Peru – Pharmaceutical Retail Market Summary (2025)

Market Potential

- Valued at approx. USD 3 billion (2023), with high dependence on imported generics.

Regulatory Landscape

- Overseen by DIGEMID; drug registration is relatively accessible, especially for non-biological generics.

Key Opportunities

- Increasing demand for affordable treatment options in the wake of healthcare reform.
- Public procurement processes favour low-cost suppliers.

Challenges

- Growing competition from Asian and Latin American suppliers.
- Currency volatility impacts margins.

Success Factors

- Invest in Spanish-language branding and local marketing.
- Supply cardiovascular, antibiotic, and oncology generics.
- Partner with private distributors and regional pharmacy chains.

Nigerian – Pharmaceutical Retail Market Summary (2025)

Market Overview

- Market Size & Growth: Nigeria's pharmaceutical market is experiencing significant growth, with a strategic goal to capture 15% of Africa's pharmaceutical market share by 2030.
- Import Dependency: Despite growth, Nigeria remains heavily reliant on imported medicines and active pharmaceutical ingredients (APIs).
- Inflation Impact: High inflation and currency devaluation have led to substantial increases in medicine prices, impacting affordability.

Healthcare Access & Infrastructure

- Universal Health Coverage: Nigeria is working towards expanding healthcare access, with initiatives aimed at improving the availability of essential medicines.
- Infrastructure Development: The government is investing in pharmaceutical-grade warehouses across multiple states to enhance drug storage and distribution.

Regulatory Environment

- NAFDAC Oversight: The National Agency for Food and Drug Administration and Control (NAFDAC) has implemented stringent regulations, including mandatory bioequivalence studies for generic medicines and enhanced traceability requirements to combat counterfeit drugs.
- Quality Standards: NAFDAC mandates that APIs and excipients used in pharmaceutical products meet international quality standards, such as those from the European Pharmacopoeia and WHO-listed authorities.

Opportunities for New Entrants

- Local Manufacturing Push: The government aims to increase local pharmaceutical production to meet at least 70% of domestic demand by 2030, presenting opportunities for investment in manufacturing facilities.
- Public-Private Partnerships: Collaborations with international organizations, such as the US Pharmacopeial Convention, are enhancing local drug production capabilities and regulatory oversight.
- Job Creation: The pharmaceutical sector is expected to create thousands of new jobs, contributing to economic growth and development.

Challenges

- Regulatory Compliance: Navigating Nigeria's evolving regulatory landscape requires a thorough understanding of NAFDAC's requirements and processes.
- Infrastructure Limitations: Despite investments, challenges remain in ensuring consistent drug quality and distribution, particularly in rural areas.
- Market Competition: The presence of both local and international pharmaceutical companies intensifies competition, necessitating strategic market entry approaches.

Strategic Recommendations

- Establish Local Partnerships: Collaborate with Nigerian pharmaceutical firms to leverage existing infrastructure and navigate regulatory requirements effectively.
- Monitor Market Dynamics: Stay informed about economic indicators, such as inflation and currency fluctuations, to adjust pricing and supply chain strategies accordingly.

Indonesian – Pharmaceutical Retail Market Summary (2025)

Market Overview

- Market Size: The value of Indonesia's pharmaceutical market is estimated to be around USD 10–12 billion, the largest in Southeast Asia.
- Generic Drug Segment: Indonesia's generic drug market is expected to register a CAGR of 8.2% during the period 2024–2032.
- Growth Drivers: These consist of a rising population, rising healthcare awareness, and governmental efforts to enhance healthcare access.

Healthcare System & Access

- National Health Insurance (JKN): Indonesia's JKN scheme is designed to achieve universal health coverage, which in turn raises demand for low-cost generic medicines.
- Healthcare Expenditures: Increasing GDP per capita, amounting to USD 4,788 in 2022, supports increased public expenditure in healthcare infrastructure.

Regulatory Environment

- Regulatory Agency: The National Agency of Drug and Food Control (BPOM) reviews and approves drugs for their safety and effectiveness.
- Recent Regulations: BPOM Regulation No. 8 of 2024 updated clinical trial approval procedures, aiming to streamline the process for pharmaceutical products.
- Health Omnibus Law: Government Regulation No. 28 of 2024 enacts the Health Omnibus Law, offering an expansive health regulation framework.

Opportunities for New Entrants

- Local Production: The policy to encourage generic drugs and biosimilars by the administration prompts local drug manufacturers to increase their manufacturing scale.
- Increasing demand for healthcare services and a growing population translate to strong opportunities for generic drug companies.
- Strategic partnerships: Local firms can assist with market entry as well as compliance with the regulatory environment.

Challenges to Consider

- Regulatory Compliance: Obtaining approval from BPOM involves careful compliance and knowledge of the local regulations.
- Infrastructural constraints: Access to distant and rural locations is logistically challenging, making strong distribution channels necessary.
- Market Competition: Established local firms such as Kalbe Farma and Kimia Farma add to market competition in the generic drug market.

Strategic Recommendations

- Regulatory Approach: Work collaboratively with BPOM to facilitate approval processes and compliance with domestic regulations.
- Local Partnerships: Leverage existing local distributors and healthcare providers to drive increased market penetration.
- Product Portfolio: Emphasise high-priority therapeutic classes and maintain a balance of plain generics and biosimilars to address differentiated market demands.
- Educational Campaigns: Organize efforts to inform healthcare professionals and consumers about the effectiveness as well as the safety of generic medicines.

MEXICO'S – PHARMACEUTICAL RETAIL MARKET SUMMARY (2025)

Market Overview

- Market Size: The Mexican generic drug market reached USD 7.4 billion in 2024 and is projected to grow at a CAGR of 5.25%, reaching USD 12.1 billion by 2033.
- Pharmaceutical Industry: Mexico's pharmaceutical sector had total revenues of USD 25.5 billion in 2022, with a CAGR of 7.8% from 2017 to 2022.
- Employment: The industry employs approximately 52,500 people, highlighting its economic significance.

Healthcare System & Access

- Coverage: Approximately 90% of Mexico's population has access to core health services through public and private systems.
- Out-of-Pocket Expenditure: Despite high coverage, out-of-pocket payments account for over 40% of total healthcare spending, indicating a demand for affordable medication options.

Regulatory Environment

- COFEPRIS: The Federal Commission for the Protection against Sanitary Risk (COFEPRIS) oversees drug approvals, ensuring safety and efficacy.
- Policy Initiatives: The government has implemented policies to promote the use of generic drugs, aiming to enhance accessibility and reduce healthcare costs.

Opportunities for New Entrants

- Market Growth: The expanding generic drug market presents opportunities for companies offering cost-effective and high-quality medications.
- Therapeutic Areas: Focus on chronic diseases, which are prevalent and require long-term medication, can be a strategic entry point.
- Manufacturing Base: Mexico offers a strong manufacturing base for pharmaceuticals, including antibiotics and analgesics, which can be leveraged for production and distribution.

Challenges to Consider

- Brand Preference: The Mexican market traditionally favors branded products over generics, necessitating efforts to build trust in generic alternatives.
- Regulatory Compliance: Navigating COFEPRIS regulations requires thorough understanding to ensure timely product approvals.
- Distribution Logistics: Efficient distribution networks are essential to reach diverse regions, especially considering the country's geography and infrastructure.

Strategic Recommendations

- Local Partnerships: Collaborate with local distributors and healthcare providers to enhance market penetration and build brand recognition.
- Educational Campaigns: Implement initiatives to educate healthcare professionals and consumers about the efficacy and safety of generic medicines.
- Regulatory Strategy: Engage with regulatory bodies early in the product development process to streamline approvals and ensure compliance.

Brazil's – Pharmaceutical Retail Market Summary (2025)

How the Industry Works

- Brazil's pharmaceutical market is the largest in Latin America, with generics holding over 35% of market volume. Governed by ANVISA, Brazil mandates stringent bioequivalence and GMP compliance for generics.
- The public healthcare system (SUS) and the Farmácia Popular program drive mass-scale access via subsidized generic drugs.
- Key players include EMS Pharma, Eurofarma, and Hypera Pharma, dominating through efficient local distribution and pricing strategies.

Current Gaps in the Market

- 85%+ API dependence on imports makes the supply chain vulnerable and expensive.
- Slow regulatory timelines (18–30 months) hinder fast generic launches.
- Consumer skepticism persists in certain regions, slowing full adoption of generics.

What Can Be Improved

- Develop domestic API production hubs to stabilize input costs.
- Introduce fast-track pathways for low-risk generics already approved by FDA/EMA.
- Launch community education campaigns to increase confidence in generics among patients and prescribers.

Opportunities for New Entrants

- Focus on underserved therapeutic niches like chronic diseases, pediatrics, and elderly care.
- Partner with regional distributors to overcome Brazil's vast geographic barriers.
- Invest in digital-first field reps and CRM tools to drive targeted prescription growth.
- Secure placement in government procurement programs to ensure consistent demand.

Consumer Expectations

- Affordable, clinically effective, and clearly labeled medication.
- Availability at local pharmacies, not just urban centers.
- Trust in the brand's reliability and transparency.

Becoming a People's Brand

- Sponsor health check-up camps and free clinics in underserved communities.
- Use WhatsApp/SMS outreach to connect and educate patients.
- Train pharmacy-based educators to promote generic usage and build trust at the point of sale.

Exporters' Strategic Notes

- Brazil can be a launchpad for LATAM expansion.
- Focus on international regulatory approvals, tiered pricing models, and localized packaging for other emerging markets.

Final Insight

- A company like Zota Healthcare (Dava India) can thrive in Brazil
- by focusing on high-efficiency manufacturing, regulatory diligence, public engagement, and
- brand trust-building—delivering truly accessible healthcare at scale.

Colombian – Pharmaceutical Retail Market Summary (2025)

Market Snapshot

- Colombia's pharmaceutical market reached USD 4.1 billion in 2021 and is projected to grow steadily to USD 10.4 billion by 2035, with a CAGR of 7.24%.
- As the third-largest pharma market in Latin America, after Brazil and Mexico, Colombia holds strategic value due to its population of 52+ million and improving access to healthcare.
- Generics are a central part of its national medicine policy.

Healthcare Access & Affordability

- Universal Health Coverage: Over 96% of the Colombian population is insured through government and private schemes.
- Low Out-of-Pocket Costs: Only 16% of total healthcare expenditure comes directly from patients – among the lowest in LATAM.
- This favours government procurement and public tenders, where cost-effective generics are essential.

Regulation & Compliance

- INVIMA (National Institute for Food and Drug Surveillance) is the regulatory body overseeing approvals.
- Colombia has robust quality controls and market segmentation for essential and generic drugs.
- Regulatory timelines can be long, but strategic engagement with INVIMA can reduce bottlenecks.

Opportunities for Market Entrants

- Generic Medicine Demand: High for chronic diseases – cardiovascular, respiratory, infectious diseases, and diabetes.
- Retail Pharmacies Dominate: These are the key channels, offering a direct pathway to patients.
- Decentralized Market: Colombia's Herfindahl-Hirschman Index (HHI) is below 1,000, meaning high competition and opportunity for disruption.
- Trusted Indian Brands have a strong opportunity due to Colombia's openness to international quality-certified players.

Key Challenges

- Regulatory Delays: INVIMA's review and certification processes can be time-consuming without local expertise.
- Brand Trust: Despite a price-sensitive population, there's still scepticism toward new generic entrants.
- Distribution: Reaching rural and remote regions is a logistical challenge – requiring strong in-country partnerships.

Strategic Playbook

- Partner with Local Distributors: Essential for understanding INVIMA, navigating customs, and building supply chains.
- Invest in Education: Train pharmacists, physicians, and the public on efficacy and quality of generics.
- Leverage WHO/USFDA/EMA Certification: These are respected by Colombian regulators and health systems.
- Prioritize Essential Drugs List: Position products already present in Colombia's POS (Plan Obligatorio de Salud) for fast adoption.
- Target Institutional Sales: Participate in government tenders and social security procurement drives.

Final Takeaway

- Colombia offers an attractive, fast-growing, price-conscious market for generic medicine manufacturers.
- By addressing regulatory hurdles, building strong local relationships, and emphasizing affordability and quality, companies like Zota Healthcare can become household names in Colombia's public and private sectors.

A Different Global Framework

When boards and investors sit down to discuss growth, the conversation rarely begins with geography. It starts with a different set of questions—practical, sometimes uncomfortable ones.

How stable is the regulatory environment, really? Not just on paper, but in day-to-day decisions.

Who pays for treatment, and how dependable is that payment system over time?

Where is value actually created in this market—through innovation, scale, access, or execution?

How long does it take to reach patients in practice, not in regulatory theory?

And finally, what happens if we get it wrong?

Traditional narratives are good at describing markets. They are far less effective at explaining how markets behave under pressure. They do not tell you how a system reacts when budgets tighten, public sentiment turns, policy priorities shift, or a launch does not go as planned.

This framework was developed to support clearer judgment around a small number of critical leadership decisions:

Where to invest—and where not to.

How to sequence expansion rather than trying to do everything at once.

How to balance growth ambitions with risk and durability.

What kind of organisation, leadership style, and operating model is actually required in each market?

In short, it is designed to help leaders make fewer avoidable mistakes.

From Geography to Behavioural Clusters

The central idea behind this Global Overview is simple: Markets should be grouped by how they behave, not where they sit on a map.

In practice, pharmaceutical markets cluster naturally around a limited number of structural factors. These factors shape incentives, constrain choices, and influence outcomes regardless of culture or location.

This book, therefore, introduces the idea of different countries, groups of markets that share similar characteristics across five core dimensions:

1. Regulation
2. Funding model
3. Market maturity
4. Access dynamics
5. Risk profile

Market Size and Forecasts

The global retail pharmacy market forms part of the broader global pharmacy industry, which includes prescription drug sales, OTC medicines, pharmacy services, and online distribution channels. Multiple industry estimates suggest substantial scale and projected growth in the coming decade.

According to an industry analysis, the global pharmacy market was valued at approximately USD 1.35 trillion in 2024, with expectations to grow to around USD 2.06 trillion by 2030 at a compound annual growth rate (CAGR) of approximately 7.3%. (Grand View Research) Other forecasts present alternative sizing: one study projected that the global retail pharmacy market would be valued at roughly USD 1,938 billion in 2025 and grow to over USD 3,219 billion by 2034 at a CAGR of 5.8%. (Custom Market Insights)

Broader sources, including retail and associated segments, suggest even larger totals. For example, estimates place the global pharmacy market at over USD 2 trillion in 2023, with potential to expand to nearly USD 3.9 trillion by 2032, backed by a forecast CAGR of over 7%. (Fortune Business Insights) These variations in market sizing reflect differences in scope (e.g., included products, services, and channel definitions) and forecast methodologies. Still, all indicate strong growth prospects for retail pharmacy over the next decade.

Within this global landscape, retail pharmacy represents the largest segment of the overall market, driven by persistent demand for prescription medicines, widespread chronic disease prevalence, ageing populations, and expansion of pharmacy services beyond mere dispensing. (Grand View Research).

Market Composition

The global pharmacy market displays clear concentrations, shaped by health system structures, population size, healthcare spending, and consumer behaviour.

North America, particularly the United States, remains the dominant region in terms of market value. North America accounted for the majority share of pharmacy revenue in recent assessments, with the U.S. contributing the largest single national market. (Custom Market Insights)

Europe and the Asia-Pacific are significant and growing markets, reflecting rising healthcare access in developing economies and continued chronic disease prevalence in established markets. (Custom Market Insights)

Emerging regions such as Latin America, the Middle East, and Africa are exhibiting differentiated growth dynamics, often constrained by infrastructure and financing realities but propelled by rising demand for essential medicines and expanding retail networks. (Custom Market Insights)

These patterns influence the competitive landscape, investment flows, distribution models, and the expansion of digital pharmacy initiatives.

Retail Pharmacy Within Healthcare Spending

Understanding retail pharmacy's role necessitates situating it within broader health expenditure patterns.

In the Organisation for Economic Co-operation and Development (OECD) countries, retail pharmaceutical spending, defined as medicines dispensed outside of hospital and inpatient settings, accounted for approximately one-sixth of total health expenditure in 2023.

On a per-capita basis, average retail pharmaceutical expenditure across OECD nations was about USD 766 (adjusted for purchasing power) in 2023, with the U.S. exhibiting the highest per-capita spending at over USD 1,700. A notable portion of this expenditure pertains to prescription drugs, which generally account for more than 75% of total retail pharmaceutical spending in most OECD countries.

The share of retail pharmacy expenditure financed by public insurance or government schemes varies widely across health systems. In many European markets, public funding covers the majority of outpatient medicine costs. In contrast, in other systems, a significant portion is financed by out-of-pocket payments, co-payments, or private insurance. These structural differences affect retail pricing strategies, consumer access, and the competitive environment among pharmacies.

source: (OECD)

Distribution Channels: Brick & Mortar vs Digital

While traditional pharmacy outlets remain the backbone of retail market access, digital pharmacy and ePharmacy platforms have grown substantially, particularly as broader digital health adoption has accelerated.

Industry analysis suggests that the global ePharmacy segment is a notable growth area, with dedicated online pharmacy platforms emerging across major markets. (Grand View Research) Although precise global revenue breakdowns vary by source, it is clear that online channels, including home delivery and click-and-collect services, are reshaping consumer access patterns, particularly for chronic therapy refills, OTC products, and wellness goods.

This digital expansion, while more robust in developed markets with high internet penetration, is also informing hybrid retail models in emerging economies, where physical outlets and online fulfilment co-exist.

Workforce Dynamics and Service Delivery

A substantial global workforce of trained pharmacists and support staff underpins retail pharmacy. According to the International Pharmaceutical Federation (FIP), over 5.5 million pharmacists are licensed or registered worldwide, based on data covering 83 countries and approximately 71% of the global population.

Workforce density varies significantly by country income level, with high-income nations maintaining markedly higher numbers of pharmacists per capita than lower-income nations.

In many systems, retail pharmacists are assuming expanded roles beyond dispensing, including patient education, chronic disease management support, immunisation services, and medication therapy reviews. These enhanced services are reshaping the traditional definition of retail pharmacy toward a more integrated health-service delivery model.

source: (fip.org)

Market Drivers and Consumer Trends

Several macro-level forces drive growth and change in the global retail pharmacy market:

Demographic Shifts: Ageing populations in both developed and emerging economies increase demand for chronic disease management, long-term medication adherence, and ancillary health services available through pharmacies. (Custom Market Insights)

Chronic Disease Prevalence: Conditions such as diabetes, cardiovascular disease, and cancer continue to require ongoing pharmacotherapy, underpinning robust prescription volumes. (Grand View Research)

Consumer Expectations: Demand for convenient access, digital fulfilment options, extended service hours, and additional health services is reshaping consumer expectations of retail pharmacy. (Custom Market Insights)

Health System Financing: Policies governing reimbursement, pricing, and pharmacy remuneration directly influence how retail pharmacies compete and serve populations. (OECD)

These consumer and system-level trends influence both the scale and nature of retail pharmacy operations globally.

Challenges and Competitive Landscape

Despite robust growth projections, the retail pharmacy sector confronts several challenges:

Regulatory and pricing pressures, particularly in markets with stringent cost controls or negotiated reimbursement frameworks, can compress margins. (OECD)

Competitive pressures from diverse players, including mass merchants, supermarket chains, and online marketplaces, intensify competition for market share and consumer engagement. (Custom Market Insights)

Workforce shortages or misalignment with service expectations can constrain the expansion of service delivery in certain geographies. (fip.org)

Nonetheless, the sector's evolution continues toward integrated care delivery, with many retail pharmacies becoming focal points for preventive care services and wellness engagement.

Closing Thoughts

Retail pharmacy sits at the heart of healthcare. It is where medicines meet people, every day, in every market. Its scale is large, shaped by population needs, funding systems, workforce capacity, and the steady shift toward digital access.

But progress in this environment is not about knowing the most markets. It is about understanding how markets behave when pressure builds, when rules tighten, costs rise, or access becomes uneven. That understanding leads to better judgment. Better judgment protects capital. And protecting capital while caring for patients is what responsible leadership looks like.

This Global Overview is meant to help build that understanding by looking beyond numbers and recognising how retail pharmacy continues to adapt, serve, and support health systems worldwide.

References Appendix (for Publishing)

Grand View Research. *Pharmacy Market Size and Share*. Grand View Research, 2025 estimate. https://www.grandviewresearch.com/industry-analysis/pharmacy-market-report (Grand View Research)

Custom Market Insights. *Global Retail Pharmacy Market 2025–2034*. https://www.custommarketinsights.com/report/retail-pharmacy-market/ (Custom Market Insights)

Fortune Business Insights. *Pharmacy Market Size, Share & Growth Outlook*. https://www.fortunebusinessinsights.com/pharmacy-market-110942 (Fortune Business Insights)

OECD. *Health at a Glance 2025 – Pharmaceutical Expenditure and Retail Medicines*. OECD Publishing; 2025. https://www.oecd.org/en/publications/2025/11/health-at-a-glance-2025_a894f72e/full-report/ (OECD)

International Pharmaceutical Federation. *Global Pharmacy Workforce Factsheet*. https://www.fip.org/files/content/getinvolved/wpd2025/WPD_Factsheet_02.pdf (fip.org)

IQVIA Institute. *The Global Use of Medicines Outlook Through 2029*. https://www.iqvia.com/insights/the-iqvia-institute/reports-and-publications/reports/the-global-use-of-medicines-outlook-through-2029 (iqvia.com)

www.ingramcontent.com/pod-product-compliance
Lightning Source LLC
LaVergne TN
LVHW070946210926
848482LV00002B/115

* 9 7 9 8 9 0 2 9 6 4 4 6 9 *